Edith Otero Quezada, Vanessa Lara Ullrich (eds.)
Marx's Others

Experiencing Gender | Volume 3

Editorial

The series **Gender as Experience** brings together monographs and edited collections that explore the constitution and transformation of gendered modes of existence from an interdisciplinary gender studies perspective. A particular focus of the series is to illuminate the contours of a critical practice of gender studies that is interested in the experiences that people have with their gender in social contexts and in the entanglement with other dimensions of their existence, through the interplay of different disciplinary perspectives such as sociology, literary studies, political science, health studies, American studies, sports science, or historical studies, among others.

The series is edited by Tomke König, Walter Erhart, Oliver Flügel-Martinsen, Valerie Kastrup and Petra Kolip.

Edith Otero Quezada is a PhD candidate in InterAmerican Studies and research associate at the Interdisciplinary Center for Gender Research (IZG) at Universität Bielefeld. She was a scholarship holder of the Rosa Luxemburg Stiftung (2017-2020). Her research interests are feminist epistemologies, political subjectivity, guerrillas and social movements, especially in Central America and Latin America.
Vanessa Lara Ullrich is a PhD candidate in political theory and the history of ideas and research associate at the Interdisciplinary Center for Gender Research (IZG) at Universität Bielefeld. She studied psychology and politics at Goethe-Universität Frankfurt (B.Sc.) and the University of Oxford (M.Sc.). Her main research interests are critical theory and social philosophy. She also writes for newspaper outlets such as "Jacobin" or "Zeit Online".

Edith Otero Quezada, Vanessa Lara Ullrich (eds.)
Marx's Others
Bodies, Affects and Experience

[transcript]

We acknowledge support for the publication costs by the Open Access Publication Fund of Bielefeld University and the Deutsche Forschungsgemeinschaft (DFG). The publication of this volume was made possible thanks to the generous support of the DFG Research Training Group "Experiencing Gender. Constitution and Transforming of Being in the World" and the Interdisciplinary Center for Gender Research (IZG), Bielefeld University.

Bibliographic information published by the Deutsche Nationalbibliothek
The Deutsche Nationalbibliothek lists this publication in the Deutsche Nationalbib-liografie

This work is licensed under the Creative Commons Attribution 4.0 (BY) license, which means that the text may be remixed, transformed and built upon and be copied and redistributed in any medium or format even commercially, provided credit is given to the author.

Creative Commons license terms for re-use do not apply to any content (such as graphs, figures, photos, excerpts, etc.) not original to the Open Access publication and further permission may be required from the rights holder. The obligation to research and clear permission lies solely with the party re-using the material.

First published in 2025 by transcript Verlag, Bielefeld
© Edith Otero Quezada, Vanessa Lara Ullrich (eds.)

transcript Verlag | Hermannstraße 26 | D-33602 Bielefeld | live@transcript-verlag.de

Cover layout: Maria Arndt, Bielefeld
Proofread: Anke Kubitza, Inka Stock, Laura Löhning, Richard Nice and Kerstin Trimble
Printed by: Majuskel Medienproduktion GmbH, Wetzlar
https://doi.org/10.14361/9783839468357
Print-ISBN: 978-3-8376-6835-3
PDF-ISBN: 978-3-8394-6835-7
ISSN of series: 2941-4059
eISSN of series: 2941-4067

Contents

Acknowledgements
Edith Otero Quezada & Vanessa Lara Ullrich 7

Introduction: Marx's Others
Vanessa Lara Ullrich 9

Part I
Political Subjects

Withering the State Machine
Lola Olufemi 25

Inverting Marxism
Jules Joanne Gleeson 43

**Rethinking Marx with(in) Latin American Societies.
A Conversation with Verónica Gago**
Edith Otero Quezada 53

Part II
Embodied Subjects

**Another Pregnancy is Possible: Making Surrogacy
Unthinkable (by Universalising Surrogacy)**
Sophie Lewis 69

Alienation in Christian Schmacht's *Fleisch mit weißer Soße* (2017)
Ivo Zender 81

Affective Becoming, Affective Belonging: A Queer Phenomenological Account of the Social Reproduction of Bodies
Jannis Ruhnau 99

Contributors 117

Acknowledgements

Edith Otero Quezada & Vanessa Lara Ullrich

This volume is the result of many exchanges. It was born from a workshop with the title "Confronting the Spectres of Marxism", which took place at the University of Bielefeld on 13th-14th October 2022. We organised this workshop together with our colleague Annika Klanke as part of a broader exchange within the research cluster "Experiencing Gender", whose home is the University of Bielefeld in Germany. We, the editors of this book, believed that a Marxist framework could help us better understand the experience of gender in contemporary capitalism. Yet, this view was not shared by everyone from the outset. Concerns of various sorts were voiced, some more theoretical in nature (Isn't Marx reductive?), others more practical (Doing something on Marx will kill your career!). We discussed these spectres of Marxism and how to confront them during two intense workshop days. This book benefited tremendously from the thought-provoking discussions with our workshop guests, Ashley Bohrer, Tithi Bhattacharya, Jules Joanne Gleeson, Lola Olufemi and Nat Raha. Our profound thanks to them. We also owe a huge debt to all of our colleagues of the research cluster "Experiencing Gender" for their support and intellectual guidance, their curiosity and generosity in engaging with this project – in particular to Prof. Tomke König and Prof. Oliver Flügel-Martinsen for their mentorship, and for initially proposing the idea of an anthology. Anke Kubitza, Inka Stock, Laura Löhning, Richard Nice, and Kerstin Trimble were of invaluable help in the process of editing and finalising the manuscript. We also wish to thank the Open Access Publication Fund of the University of Bielefeld, the Deutsche Forschungsgemeinschaft (DFG), the Research Training Group "Experiencing Gender" and the Interdisziplinäres Zentrum für Geschlechterforschung (IZG) for their financial support, through which we hope to make the volume more accessible beyond the confines of academia. Above all, our deep gratitude goes to our contributors, who not only delivered astute texts and interviews but also enriched our thinking throughout the process of producing this volume.

Introduction: Marx's Others

Vanessa Lara Ullrich

"Was Marx right after all?" reads the headline of the German magazine *Der Spiegel* in 2022. A bushy-bearded Karl Marx winks from the cover, wearing a green T-shirt emblazoned with a windmill. The image belongs to an article that nonchalantly resurrects Marx for the oxymoron "green capitalism". *Der Spiegel* is not alone in its bold appropriation of Marx: in the same year, the *Financial Times* heralded "'Degrowth' – Marxism is Back for the Modern Age"; in 2018, *The Economist* proclaimed: "Rulers of the World: Read Karl Marx!" and the *Teen Vogue* magazine ran the headline: "Who is Karl Marx: Meet the Anti-Capitalist Scholar".

These are just a few examples of a wider trend: Marx has made his way back into the mainstream after being considered an irrelevant theorist at best and a taboo at worst for decades. The more capitalist crisis wreaks havoc, the more people seem to call themselves Marxists. Many, understandably, are outraged by the crises of our contemporary moment: climate disaster, imperialist warfare, far-right radicalisation and militarised borders against refugees and migrants. But to reduce Marx to moral outrage is to forfeit his power as a dialectical thinker. His key insight was not that capitalism is evil. It was that capitalism is a social relation – and as such could be changed.

That said, we cannot straightforwardly apply his more than 170-year-old texts to our fundamentally transformed world. Can we return to Marx today, and is Marxism as a political project still appropriate for the times in which we live? A glimpse into Marxist history is instructive: the question of how to update and develop Marx has plagued Marxists ever since the German SPD started codifying Marxist theses as revolutionary theory. In response, the philosopher Georg Lukács argued for a focus on method, not just content. Genuine Marxist critique, he insisted in 1919, is not "the exegeses of a 'sacred book'" (1971: 1), it can even "dismiss all of Marx's theses" (ibid: 1) – except for, and this is crucial, the "dialectical method" (ibid) that Marx had adopted from Hegel.

This anthology, too, seeks to rework Marxist critique for the twenty-first century, using a dialectical approach.[1] But its subject is a different one: the worker in this book is no longer only the Fordist assembly line worker, but today's fragmented assemblage of racialised and gendered workers whose *bodies, affects and experience* this volume centres as material relations through which sexuality, "race" and gender are lived and enacted every day.

The problem with studying the experiences of this fragmented subject, however, is that we are still stuck in the false choice between vulgar Marxism and identity politics. Both are essentialising in that they assume the possibility of unmediated experiences. Vulgar Marxism, the Stalinist offspring of Marxism, assumes that workers have revolutionary consciousness simply because they experience alienation every day. What makes it vulgar is that it derives consciousness from the worker's social position, or to put it in Marxist terminology, the "political superstructure" from the "economic foundation" (Marx 1859: 263). This reductive and deterministic logic renders "race", gender and sexuality secondary to what is considered the primary economic contradiction of class. Despite its different premises, identity politics also centres experiences of oppression as the source of social identity, thus fragmenting people into different groups with shared interests which need to be protected through individual rights. Yet, in doing so, identity politics only ends up making everyone equal in the "dull compulsion" (Marx 1867: 726), as Marx put it, to sell their labour power.

This volume rejects this false binary by building on both older Marxian genealogies of thinking about sexuality, "race" and gender and more recent revivals (cf. Lewis 2022 [2016]; Gleeson/O'Rourke 2021). In fact, Marxism already has a rich tradition – think of August Bebel, Rosa Luxemburg or Frantz Fanon – that rejected a simplistic economic determinism and took seriously the imbrication of capitalist society with racism and patriarchy. In that sense, this tradition is closer to Marx, who posited the need for political mediation between concrete experience and class consciousness, between the *base* and the *superstructure*.

---

1   I am deeply indebted to Ilya Afanasyev, Edith Otero Quezada, Leila Ullrich and Michael Schwind for patiently reading drafts of this introduction, sharing their thoughts and providing invaluable comments.

Building on that tradition and its emphasis on politics, the key contribution of this book is to link the experiences of racialised and gendered subjects with the challenge of forging a collective political subject under the current version of capitalism. This is important precisely because immediate experiences of subordination do not automatically translate into revolutionary subjectivity. Marx himself did not think they would – otherwise he probably would not have devoted thousands of pages to the critical task of welding workers into a revolutionary movement. But while Marx wrote at a time of an active socialist movement, which he both fiercely criticised and supported, today we lack a transnational organisation among workers.

Who then are the political subjects capable of changing our world today? Is it still the proletariat, as Marx envisaged? Is it social movements? The question of the subject, in its current form, poses a dilemma: on the one hand, we cannot return to Marx's premise of an organised global working class as the political subject, which is difficult to achieve in our present moment. On the other hand, as the philosopher Holly Lewis cautions, we should not substitute the proletariat "for any oppressed population" (Lewis 2022 [2016]: 71). By neglecting class analysis, this move would shift "socialist politics from the political to the moral" (ibid), leaving us with a mere moral critique of oppression. The question of the revolutionary subject therefore requires rethinking, as today's dispersed and divided workforce no longer corresponds to the type of worker Marx encountered in his time. Edith Otero Quezada's interview with Verónica Gago, for example, focuses on labouring and revolutionary subjects in light of the shifting dynamics of capitalism and the way in which they are shaped by new forms of debt and profit extraction.

The subject, therefore, is the central concern of this book. The book asks: how can the embodied subject transform into a political subject? It answers: we cannot know, but we have to learn from the history of Marxist struggles. It deals with the subject in two senses: first, the embodied subject and how it experiences and is affected by the world, and second, the political subject and the question of its transformative power. We examine how these two subjects can be further fleshed out through Black feminist, queer and trans theory. Their strength is that they start from embodied subjects, deepening Marx's idea of the labouring subject, defined by the "productive expenditure of human brains, nerves, and muscles" (Marx 1867: 54), which forms its connective tissue with the world. Rather than discussing whether these theories and Marxism are commensurable, this volume shows that together they can help us to study bodies, affects and experience under contemporary capitalism.

Crossing disciplinary boundaries, this book draws on cultural and literary studies, philosophy, political theory and sociology, its material coming from novels, archives and interviews amongst others. Our contributors work at the intersection of art, academia and activism, and think at the intersection of Marxism, Black feminist, queer and trans theory. Each offers their own reading of Marx. What unites them is a commitment to Marx's imperative to overcome all relations that keep people in bondage. They re-engage with tenets of Marx's theory that, with few exceptions, have been declared obsolete as post-structuralism and post-Marxism won intellectual ground. But just at the moment when all Marxist thinking was proclaimed outdated, it began to haunt us. We cannot yet move beyond Marxism. Theories that claim the opposite, such as Chantal Mouffe and Ernesto Laclau's *Hegemony and Socialist Strategy* (2001), risk detaching "the political" from economic relations and reducing politics to discourse. But the volume does not return to the reductive and economistic version of Marxism that Mouffe and Laclau rightly criticised. Instead, it returns to 1) the embodied and 2) the political subject, which I will now discuss in more detail.

1. The Embodied Subject

Embodied subjects and their everyday experiences are the first key concern of the book. This is important, because it is subjects that make history, even if, as Marx famously wrote, they do so not under circumstances of their own choosing. While this sounds simple enough, Marx himself abstracts from subjective experience, stating right at the beginning of *Capital Volume I* that he will analyse individuals "only in so far as they are the personifications of economic categories" (Marx 1867: 10). Although Marx is far from the reductive thinker he is often caricatured as, there are undoubtedly deterministic versions of Marxism that erase the subject in the supposedly lawlike motion of history. But to think that we can make sense of the world through subjective experience is equally reductive. Far from it: subject-centred approaches only take us so far, because the abstract mechanisms through which capitalist society operates are not directly accessible through concrete experience.

While individuals enter Marx's magnum opus *Capital* only as carriers of economic relations, Lea Ypi's *Free* discovers "the flesh and blood of a real person" lurking "behind every personification of an economic category" (2021: 308). Socialism, Ypi writes, "is above all a theory of human freedom, of how to think about progress in history" (ibid: 305) – a reading that places Marx in the lineage of radical bourgeois thinkers such as Rousseau, Kant and Hegel. Like Ypi, we focus on flesh-and-blood subjects. And like Ypi, we are mindful about the political appropriations of the idea of progress given their tendency to disavow the role of human subjects in shaping the course of history. After all, the subject and its passions occupy an ambiguous place in a teleological philosophy of history such as Marx's and Hegel's. Postmodern intellectuals have even dismissed the idea of progress altogether (cf. Lyotard 1984), worrying that it grinds subjects in the mills of history. Hegel's world spirit (*Weltgeist*), the movement of reason in history, they claim, devoured the unconscious, particular desires of the individual and disgorged them as conscious, universal reason. It turned people into material and walked over dead bodies.

Yet the opposite is true. Hegel's *Lectures on the Philosophy of World History* emphasise the concrete actions, aspirations and desires of the individual subject in moving history forward: "*Nothing great* has been accomplished in the world *without passion*" (2011: 92–93; original emphasis), Hegel tells us. Indeed, these passions and desires form the engine through which the spirit realises itself in the direction of freedom. Yet, this idea of embodied human progress, as is well known, was perverted by Stalinism almost a century later. Its doctrine that everyone must bleed for socialist progress rationalised all violence *post festum*. It repressed the thinking and acting subject.

By contrast, the authors in this collection build on those critical traditions that recover the embodied, affective and experiencing subject from Marxist history. They explore, for example, the relation of Black feminist abolitionism to Marx's, Engels' and Lenin's reflections on the dictatorship of the proletariat (Lola Olufemi); they envision an alternative pregnancy, challenging genetic parenthood and the nuclear family in the context of what is a growing global surrogacy industry (Sophie Lewis), they analyse the affective dimension of alienation (Ivo Zender) and the class struggle of trans workers (Jules Joanne Gleeson).

Thinking about bodies, affects and experiences from a Marxist perspective is complicated by two considerations. First, reified notions of bodies, affects and experience as metaphysical matter, such as those prevalent in some strands of phenomenological, psychological and new materialist research (cf. Massumi 1995: 91), should have no place in Marxism. But can one argue that embodied experiences are historical and social, that they are not some simple manifestations of some fixed inner "truth", and still postulate some truthfulness and agency at this level? And can we then avoid the trap of ahistorical primordialism and essentialism? Second, how can we think about bodies, affects and experience in dialectical terms, that is, without collapsing the subject and object, the social and psychological, the individual and society?

On the face of it, there seems to be a contradiction between a Marxist-Hegelian dialectical method and a phenomenological approach centring on bodies, affects and experience. For Hegel, our experiences and senses do not give us immediate access to truth: what appears as brute fact is already a standpoint mediated by a subject (Hegel 1979: 64–65). This is why sensuous experience alone gets us only so far in grasping the contradictions of capitalist society. Marx shows this in *Capital* (1867) where he begins with what we can feel and perceive about the commodity (the particular), but ends with what we cannot see, its value (the universal), moving from the immediate appearance of the commodity to its content.

Similarly, the contributions to this volume begin with particular experiences of "race", gender and sexuality, but then analyse how they are mediated by capitalist society – their key point being that gender and "race" are also the social ties of capitalist society that make it work rather than some separate social forms that just happen to coexist with capitalist relations. Bourgeois society, for example, tells us that "sex" is the biological division of people into men and women, which goes hand in hand with specific social attributes. But if we place "sex" in its historical context rather than freezing it at a particular point in time, its content reveals itself: what appears as a biological division is in fact a social division of labour, inextricably linked to the mechanisms of capitalist production and reproduction (cf. Vogel 1983; Federici 2004; Fraser 2014).

Even though contemporary capitalism does not seem to operate strictly in line with the gender binary anymore, it still feeds on forms of oppression that feminise certain bodies, while simultaneously blurring these distinctions and incorporating queer and trans workers into its exploitative relations. No doubt, if capital can make value out of queerness and diversity, it will; what matters is the creation of value, not what creates it. But how can we recognise at once that capitalism can adapt and appropriate without returning to the logic of the main economic contradiction, rendering gendered and racialised contradictions secondary?

The volume opposes the Stalinist primacy of economic determination, which sees history driven towards freedom by economic forces rather than by embodied subjects. To the contrary, freedom is painstaking work. Hegel's "slaughterhouse" (2011: 90) of history might point to a speculative challenge: if we do not realise freedom, all the sacrifices, the countless lives lost in the struggle for freedom, will have been in vain. Lea Ypi beautifully reflects on this challenge in her book on freedom:

> In some ways, I have gone full circle. When you see a system change once, it's not that difficult to believe that it can change again. Fighting cynicism and political apathy turns into what some might call a moral duty; to me, it is more of a debt that I feel I owe to all the people of the past who sacrificed everything because *they* were not apathetic, *they* were not cynical, *they* did not believe that things fall into place if you just let them take their course. If I do nothing, their efforts will have been wasted, their lives will have been meaningless. (2021: 310; original emphasis)

What makes this paragraph so evocative is that it does not place history in the past, but relates it to the present. But does Ypi reproduce the teleology of progress here? After all, this passage might sound like an expression of what one might call a Stalinist affect – perhaps, in part, explaining why so many people were persuaded and motivated by it: it is exactly the logic of not letting things just take their course, but acting in the name of both past sacrifices and future freedoms, even if it means using violence here and now. Indeed, Stalinism, though enabled by ontological and epistemological determinism, was not just determinism, but determinism combined with a belief in the select agency of the party. Arguably, the main problem with it is not that it denies the agency of actual subjects, but that it all too effectively creates a monstrous subject. What can this detour into Marxist history tell us about the possibility of welding workers into a political subject today? This is the question I examine in the next section.

2. The Political Subject

The second key concern of this volume is how subjects and their experiences can be assembled into political subjects, that is, into an organised collective movement. Put another way: how can the embodied subject transform the world politically?

For Marx, the struggle for political change is mired in contradictions: despite their struggles for better living conditions, workers kept constantly reproducing their own bondage. The main reason for their subordination was that in bourgeois consciousness, workers only appeared as the object of the production process, when in fact they were also its subject. They are the ones that get up every morning to labour, and yet the product of their labour confronts them as alien; their labour is the source of all value, and yet they appear as "a living appendage of the machine" (Marx 1867: 487). They could work less thanks to the development of the productive forces, and yet they either work themselves to death to earn a living, or are thrown out of work by the million (ibid: 411).

Marx's solution to this subject-object inversion is well known: without a political standpoint that allowed workers to understand themselves as a class, they would continually reproduce their own immiseration. Without a political subject that did not just call for socialism in the abstract, but that linked the consciousness of class relations to concrete struggles for better living conditions, they would forever orbit in a capital-driven universe.

For Marx, this political subject was not just individual workers, but workers organised in what he called *"the revolutionary dictatorship of the proletariat"* (1891: 95; original emphasis). When we hear the word *dictatorship* today, we hear the sabre-rattling of violent despots. Marx and Engels did not. Their concept of dictatorship came from the ancient Roman Republic. Crucial to this tradition of political thought was that *dictatorship* referred to a temporary form of rule by a collective subject to address a crisis (Ypi 2020: 278).

But why should a *dictatorship of the proletariat* be necessary at all – and what is the role of the state in this process? Lola Olufemi's contribution looks at this question. She argues that today's abolitionist movements, which renew the call for abolishing the state, highlight the importance of a continued engagement with the *dictatorship of the proletariat* but also its problems. Can the notion of the *dictatorship of the proletariat* inform current efforts to build a collective movement?

A digression into Marxist history is illuminating: while Hegel still believed in the state as a medium for the realisation of freedom, for Marxists and anarchists, the state, as the historically specific political form of capitalist society, was the means, to put it no doubt too simply, of one class to oppress the other. But this did not mean that the bourgeoisie could wield the state as an instrument at its own will – on the contrary, the crisis of capitalist society, its irresolvable contradictions, produce the state as an entity that becomes to some extent autonomous vis-à-vis the bourgeoisie (Marx 1852: 143). It was Vladimir Lenin who argued in *The State and Revolution* (1917) that, far from resolving the contradiction between capital and labour, the state merely prolonged its life and thus the rule of the bourgeoisie. Its function was to muffle the violent clash between capitalists and workers, not to supersede it. The point, therefore, was not for workers to win power in order to reform the state, but to abolish it along with all its violent features: prisons, police, a standing army.

But while anarchists and Marxists agreed on the need to abolish the state, they famously disagreed on how to do it: the former believed in a direct transition to a stateless society, the latter in the *dictatorship of the proletariat* as a transition phase.

Notice that dictatorship did not designate a fixed form of government. It was above all a social form that could, in principle, take different shapes. In fact, for Marx and Engels, bourgeois democracy too was a dictatorship – even more violent, because a minority oppressed the majority rather than the other way around. Except that, in reality, the dictatorship of the proletariat, established after the Russian Revolution, also turned out to be, as is well known, a minority (the party) oppressing the majority. Should that have come as a surprise? For the anarchist thinker, Mikhail Bakunin, it certainly would not have. Already in 1870, he had predicted that the dictatorship of the proletariat was bound to ossify, to become an instrument of state terror. It would not wither away. Clearly, we cannot simply retrieve Marx's dictatorship of the proletariat, nor can we ignore the anarchist critique of it.

Today, the state is once again at the centre of political critique and organising: mass incarceration, police violence, the criminalisation of climate activists and the securitisation of borders against migrants and refugees highlight the urge to confront the violence of the state. In this political climate, Black feminist abolitionism and its call for a world without prisons and the police have gained new impetus in recent years. Lola Olufemi's contribution brings Black abolitionism, which perhaps has more affinity with anarchism in its focus on building from the present, into dialogue with the dictatorship of the proletariat. It raises an unresolved problem: how can we build a radically different world without replicating forms of state power? The dictatorship of the proletariat, in its actual historical form, did not resolve this dilemma. It rather exacerbated it.

Moreover, its bloody history has added to the difficulties of forging a political subject today, as political mobilisation has shifted in response, from centralised parties to decentralised movements. Social movements are now often hailed as the new agents of change: climate movements like *Fridays for Future*, anti-racist movements like *Black Lives Matter* in the US or feminist movements like *Ni Una Menos* in Argentina. This turn to movements has gathered new steam due to the fact that left-wing parties almost all over the world have been in crisis. But the shift from parties to movements as the primary carriage of left politics raises further problems. It has contributed to the fragmentation of political subjects, organising in silos around different issues such as climate, housing or health, at the expense of strategic convergence. In the absence of an international workers' movement, Marxist theory and practice are falling further and further apart. The former is withering into academic niche products, perfectly reflecting what Marx called the separation of manual labour and intellectual labour to the point where they "become deadly foes" (Marx 1867: 509). In fact, given that intellectual labour feeds on the surplus value generated by manual labour (Luxemburg 2003: 107–108), the educated bourgeoisie actually has an interest in maintaining the capitalist relations that secure its existence. Short of an internationally organised workers' movement that can mediate between and bring together the hand and head, the particular and universal, workers have little chance of regaining intellectual planning and social control over their labour.

This is the political conjuncture out of which this volume was born, the history of Marxism weighing on its pages. The most pressing challenge today seems to be precisely how the embodied subject can transform into a political subject. These two subjects are non-identical. Exploitation does not necessarily give rise to socialist consciousness. It can produce very different forms of political consciousness, and even estrange workers from politics altogether. In the current political climate, we can only build towards both political mobilisation and a better understanding of the contemporary contours of capitalism, preparing for a moment in which revolutionary change will become possible.

3. Outline of the Book

The first part of the book brings together contributions that engage with the question of how embodied subjects can become political subjects.

The first contribution *Withering the State Machine*, by the writer Lola Olufemi, places the concept of the dictatorship of the proletariat in the context of Black abolitionist thought and practice. Olufemi updates the problem of how we can abolish the state by engaging with Marx, Engels and Lenin and bringing them into a dialogue with Black feminist voices from the archives. Following thinkers such as Walter Benjamin, she rejects a linear and progressivist philosophy that conflates history with the past. Instead, her dialectical approach allows communist struggles at different times to speak to one another in order to spark a moment of redemption in the present.

The second paper *Inverting Marxism*, by the writer and historian Jules Joanne Gleeson, centres the struggles of trans workers in the workplace, household and the clinic, focusing particularly on how the current far-right targets trans people and represents them as an ostensible threat to the nuclear family as a key site for the reproduction of capitalist social relations. Gleeson reflects on the theoretical implications of what she calls "transgender Marxism" and what it has to offer to the Marxist tradition in terms of understanding our contemporary moment by challenging the juxtaposition of identity and class politics.

Edith Otero Quezada's interview with Verónica Gago reposes the question of the revolutionary subject today. Who is that subject and what would it take for workers, reproductive workers and movements to become transnationally organised? And how can we rethink *the worker* in light of the contemporary contours of capitalism and the way in which they play out through *expanded extractivism* and dynamics of debt.

The second part on "embodied subjects" gathers three contributions that shed light on the embodied experiences of contemporary capitalism.

In the contribution *Another Pregnancy is Possible*, the writer Sophie Lewis updates the long-standing feminist critique of pregnancy as a form of labour in the context of the global exploitation of surrogacy workers. In light of the commodification of babies, Lewis explores the potential that gestational labour poses for superseding the entrenched ideology of the nuclear family and genetic parenthood, instead opening up horizons for the socialisation of childbirth and child-rearing.

Ivo Zender's text on *Alienation in Christian Schmacht's Fleisch mit weißer Soße* reinterprets Marx's concept of alienation through a literary analysis of the autofictional contemporary German novella *Fleisch mit weißer Soße (Meat with White Sauce)*. Its protagonist, Chrissy, a trans sex worker, longs for closeness to others and a radically changed world, but finds himself trapped in separation, paralysis and depression. Using literature as a tool to explore affective and embodied experience under capitalism, such as the physical and mental uniformity of capitalist labour, Zender develops an account of alienation infused with insights from phenomenology withoutsuggesting that we can return to an unalienated essence.

The last paper *Affective Becoming, Affective Belonging* by the sociologist Jannis Ruhnau, asks what it would take to bring the living individual into a critique of contemporary capitalism given that Marx does not analyse individuals in their own right, but rather treats them as carriers of economic functions. To this end, Ruhnau combines Sara Ahmed's queer phenomenology with social reproduction theory, focusing on how bodies reproduce themselves in order to labour. He interweaves these theoretical questions with empirical insights from narrative interviews to incorporate the individual and its lived experience for a deeper understanding of the contradictions of social reproduction under capitalist social relations.

References

Bakunin, Mikhail (1950): Marxism, Freedom and State, London: Freedom Press.

Der Spiegel (2022): Grüner Kapitalismus: Hatte Marx doch recht?, December 30, 2022 (https://www.spiegel.de/wirtschaft/gruener-kapitalismus-die-chance-auf-eine-nachhaltigere-wirtschaftsordnung-a-00f49cb5-6509-456f-94ad-f420fab94200).

Federici, Silvia (2004): Caliban and the Witch. Women, the Body and Primitive Accumulation, Williamsburg: Autonomedia.

Financial Times (2022): 'Degrowth' – Marxism Is Back for the Modern Age, November 6, 2022 (https://www.ft.com/content/b1a505ac-c36f-4b4d-9ab0-6f5d9d0e185d).

Fraser, Nancy (2014): "Behind Marx's Hidden Abode: For an Expanded Conception of Capitalism." In: New Left Review 86, pp. 55–60.

Gleeson, Jules Joanne/O'Rourke, Elle (eds.) (2021): Transgender Marxism, London: Pluto Press.

Hegel, Georg Wilhelm Friedrich (1979): Phenomenology of Spirit, New York: Oxford University Press.

Hegel, Georg Wilhelm Friedrich (2011): Lectures on the Philosophy of World History, Volume I: Manuscripts of the Introduction and the Lectures of 1822–1823, Oxford: Oxford University Press.

Laclau, Ernesto/Mouffe, Chantal (2001): Hegemony and Socialist Strategy: Towards a Radical Democratic Politics, London: Verso.

Lenin, Vladimir Ilyich (1992): The State and Revolution, London: Penguin Books.

Lewis, Holly (2022 [2016]): The Politics of Everybody: Feminism, Queer Theory, and Marxism at the Intersection, London, New York and Dublin: Bloomsbury Academic.

Lukács, Georg (1971): History and Class Consciousness, London: Merlin.

Luxemburg, Rosa (2003): The Accumulation of Capital, London: Routledge.

Lyotard, Jean-François (1984): The Postmodern Condition: A Report on Knowledge. Volume 10, Minneapolis: University of Minnesota Press.

Marx, Karl (2010 [1859]): A Contribution to the Critique of Political Economy, Collected Works of Marx and Engels, Volume 29, London: Lawrence and Wishart.

Marx, Karl (1996 [1867]): Capital Volume 1, Collected Works of Marx and Engels, Volume 35, London: Lawrence and Wishart.

Marx, Karl (2010 [1891]): Critique of the Gotha Programme, Collected Works of Marx and Engels, Volume 24, London: Lawrence and Wishart.

Marx, Karl (2010 [1852]): The Eighteenth Brumaire of Louis Bonaparte, Collected Works of Marx and Engels, Volume 11, London: Lawrence and Wishart.

Massumi, Brian (1995): "The Autonomy of Affect." In: Cultural critique 31, pp. 83–109.

Teen Vogue (2018): "Who Is Karl Marx: Meet the Anti-Capitalist Scholar", May 10, 2018 (https://www.teenvogue.com/story/who-is-karl-marx).

The Economist (2018): "Rulers of the World: Read Karl Marx!", May 3, 2018 (https://www.economist.com/books-and-arts/2018/05/03/rulers-of-the-world-read-karl-marx).

Vogel, Lise (1983): Marxism and the Oppression of Women: Toward a Unitary Theory, New Jersey: Rutgers University Press.

Ypi, Lea (2020): "Democratic dictatorship: Political legitimacy in Marxist perspective." In: European Journal of Philosophy, 28/2, pp. 277–291.

Ypi, Lea (2021): Free: Coming of Age at the End of History, London: Penguin Books.

Part I
Political Subjects

Withering the State Machine

Lola Olufemi

> What I did that was new was to prove:
> (1) that the existence of classes is only bound up with the particular, historical phases in the development of production (historische Entwicklungsphasen der Produktion)
> (2) that the class struggle necessarily leads to the dictatorship of the proletariat,
> (3) that this dictatorship itself only constitutes the transition to the abolition of all classes and to a classless society.

An excerpt from Karl Marx's letter to Weydemeyer dated March 5, 1852.[1]

***

Olive knew that beyond accusations of division, the black woman's position could tell them something specific about the worker and racial capitalism. Every time they were dismissed in the meetings, something inside her broke. The movement was falling apart. But it was women that kept things alive on the ground – they worked with the lawyers to get brothers out of prison, to stop deportations in action; they ran the mutual aid networks, stocked the bookshop, facilitated the meetings. Yet their strategies were picked apart, their ideas whispered between brothers' speeches.

She didn't understand how everyone else slept so soundly at night, with so much wrong with the world. Sometimes the sky in London would settle into a black so thick, so dense, it was impossible to see through. Watching it roll over the city, she would think of the global chains that connected her to other anti-colonial movements across the world. She'd never felt more power than as a squatter, firmly in the centre of an organised, relentless communist movement. They were showing the people that things could be had for free. This world wasn't about how much you owed, or keeping your head down to avoid

---

1 Marx, Karl (1975 [1852]): "Marx to Weydemeyer. Dated March 5, 1852." In: Karl Marx/ Friedrich Engels (eds.) Selected Correspondence, Moscow: Progress Publishers, p. 669.

trouble. She remembered Lenin: *So long as the state exists there is no freedom; when there is freedom, there will be no state.*

An excerpt from 'Narrative consistency' in *Experiments in Imagining Otherwise* written by Lola Olufemi, 2020.[2]

Figure 1: Sisters Uncut. Sarah Everard Demonstration, September 2021 [3]

***

A thorough assessment of the conditions in which events, rebellions and class struggle arise and a belief that consciousness must be rooted, proceeding from *somewhere* or *something* external to the self, calls on us to remember that freedom is not an abstraction. Marxism holds that the task for those concerned with ending the immiseration of the working classes, should lay in undertaking forms of historical analysis that illuminate a path for action in the contemporary moment. The effects of thinking about freedom in this manner are many; there is no doubt that the tenets of historical materialism make freedom

---

2   Olufemi, Lola (2021): Experiments in Imagining Otherwise, London: Hajar Press: 22–23.
3   See: Sisters Uncut (2021): "Sisters Uncut: 'Why We're Launching National Intervention Training after Sarah Everard's Kidnap by Cop", September 30, 2021 (https://gal-dem.com/wayne-couzens-arrested-sarah-intervention/).

attainable by uncovering the economic processes that govern social organisation over time, revealing how these processes might be jeopardized and then defeated. But a refusal to interrogate the conceptual power of 'History', how it flattens temporality into a stadial and linear teleology, risks turning freedom into a matter of prediction based on the immutability of the past and the historical narratives that produce it. This tendency erodes the need to remain flexible, expanding Marxist analysis and struggle in light of the racialised, gendered and other forms of unevenly distributed labour that occur in capitalist societies. It defangs those radical movements that seek redress for the workers crushed by these conditions.

I begin this intervention with three seemingly disconnected excerpts gathered from the detritus of 'History', all of which are concerned with forms of resistance against oppressive state forces and ultimately, I wager, the abolition of the state. Each narrates a form of principled struggle against the state apparatus that responds to the specificity of their material and temporal condition. Marx speaks to the processes through which a dictatorship of the proletariat is to be established, my fabulated account of the actions of Olive Morris attends to her role in challenging state hegemony as part of grassroots movements in London in the 1980s, and the image of organisers at a Sisters Uncut protest from 2021 represents the striking visual and aesthetic dimension of opposition to a carceral state.

Traditional Marxist approaches might designate the latter excerpts as insufficiently analytical, precisely because they concern revolutionary subjects whose analysis is inflected by critical understandings of race, gender and class but asking, 'how are Olive Morris, Sisters Uncut and Karl Marx related?' does two things. Firstly, it stays with abstraction, imagining that there might be some intangible connection (rooted in spirit, desire, what Marxists might refer to as mysticism) between these three entities, despite the different time periods in which they exist. It complicates the stadial Marxist dictum that all things must be neatly fixed inside of a History in order to be understood or capable of being analysed. This is not a new intervention; the particularity of this progressivist approach has been explicitly rejected by Marxists throughout history, my intervention is aligned with Cedric Robinson and Rosa Luxemburg whose analysis of both History and temporality stressed the agency of revolutionary subjects to challenge and escape the strictures of these concepts, and insisted on the expansion and reappropriation of these terms against capitalist accumulation. If dialectical thought encourages an embrace of the tension and conflicts located inside any totality, then I extend this disobedience theoretically. I ask, why think Marxism anew, when we could think it differently? Rather than attempting to read the actions of historical and contemporary feminist organisers like Olive Morris and Sisters Uncut in light of Marx's framework, I instead want to ask, would it be possible to make these actors speak to one another across time? I do so by grounding my analysis of these three different conjunctures of political struggle through a reading of time as foregrounded by the creative character of Walter Benjamin's *Theses on History*. What new pedagogical and political implications might this dialogue have for those interested in the project of material transformation through thought, language and most importantly, action?

Using a materialist black feminist methodology and creative practice, I want to think with Marxism *against* the weight of History, rather than conceding it as the basis from which all things must be understood. I wager that, finding the connection between Olive Morris, Sisters Uncut and Marxist thought expressed through multiple actors (here Marx, Engels and Lenin) requires us, as dialectical thinkers, to shrug off the cloak of History, to loosen it ever so slightly and allow the past and present and future to collide. By 'History' I refer to the linear and sequential events of the past which are articulated through process, occurrence and historiography that seeks to impose a narrative that explains *what was then* and subsequently, *what is now*. I am interested in the power of traditional historiography to create a two-tier system of official and unofficial events and how the authority of narrative power – the ability to define historical record – is directly correlated to bourgeois ownership.

Evading 'History' in order to read the connections in political fervency between these subjects might produce a different orientation to materialist struggle, particularly the notion of the 'future' as a fixed entity that must be 'won' or 'secured' rather than a site that is produced and reproduced in the present. I hold, in line with Walter Benjamin, that there is value in understanding the task of historical materialism as related to what Beiner (1984) calls 'a redemptive relation to the past, rather than a question of what is to come.' Benjamin is remembered as one of the most creative Marxist thinkers precisely because his *Theses on History* marries the tenets of historical materialism with a theological impulse. This move interests me because of the creativity at its core: an inventiveness that unsettles the fixity of historicism. Whilst my own concerns shy away from theology, I'm interested in disobeying the tenants of historical materialism by behaving ambivalently to the rules of History, which seek to impose a chronology of events from which political material conditions emerge and are analysed. Instead, I enact a redemptive relation to the past, by 'rescuing' Olive Morris from it and behaving as if it were possible for her to speak to Marx, Engels and Lenin and Sisters Uncut and for them to speak back.

To approach History in this manner is to critique the limitations it places on dialectical thinking and to resuscitate the affective dimensions of Marxism. As a practise based researcher and writer, I am interested in the promise of artistic approaches: how they can aid in defying capitalism by bringing a vitality and texture to resistance. Such a texture is dependent on continued experimentation with form as well as a belief in arts ability to shape political consciousness through affect. My intervention takes on an artistic character in order to emphasise the role of aesthetics in exercising the *impulse* to resist not to reaffirm a belief that artistic creation can in and of itself transform material conditions. New perspectives that claim to think through, with, against and beyond Marx frequently contend with the conferred authority of historical fact. It is a historical fact that Marx was a German man, who lived and whose works continue to provide the lifeblood for a number of ongoing theoretical and practical debates that drive class struggle against capitalist social relations. It is a historical fact that Olive Morris, South London resident, black communist and member of the Brixton Black Women's Group founded in 1973 produced knowledge that furthered Marxist thought as it pertained to the positions of black women workers in the United Kingdom. It is a historical fact that Sisters Uncut have been at the forefront of radical forms of feminist organising in the United Kingdom since 2014 and that, in challenging the corrosive effects of austerity and carceral state for working class women through direct action have provided a new way of thinking about what contemporary feminism is and *should be*.

Feminist, anti-racist, and queer approaches to Marxism alert us to the uneven, complex and differential nature of capitalist totality. They help investigate the affective impulses that make us want to analyze our conditions and fight back. They demonstrate that *everyone* has the potential to become a revolutionary subject. Understanding one of the core features of Marxism: which is to strike the heart of capitalist social and economic relations, to cede back the theoretical ground necessary to *change* History, not merely interpret it, first begins with a recognition of how History's weight can and does drag us down. It is not a contradiction to embrace the structural tenets of historical materialism whilst critiquing its approach to the past, as Benjamin did. It is also not a contradiction to insist that Marxism must continue to utilise and contend with creative methods in its analysis, paying close attention to the affective relations they produce and embodied experiences of the quotidian which are ordered by temporal regimes. Creative experimentation with temporality in Marxist analysis might bring flight to materialist political struggle weighed down by History, enrich us, help us understand how and why we struggle and ensure we do not consign ourselves to the realm of defeat.

* * *

I have placed a short extract from Marx's letter to a friend alongside my own fictional speculation of events in the life of Olive Morris because following Wilkie, Savransky and Rosengarten (2017) I believe speculation can reorder the realm of the plausible, probable and the possible. I enact this comparison for the purposes of reading the two texts together even though they exist in different spatio-temporal locations. To strip them of their context is to extract them from historical time, the time of the event and bring them into an aporetic temporality capable of holding contradiction and tracing their affective impulses.

I remake Rizvana's Bradley's concept of 'representational aporia' (2015) which she uses to analyse how black womanhood – the specific configuration of race and gender – "challenges the prescribed limits of personhood, identity and humanity" (2015: 162) and repurpose it to think about the irreconcilability, puzzlement and doubt produced by temporal play. An aporetic temporality creates an internal irresolvability that challenges the hegemony of clock-time. Temporal play is an imaginative act. Reading 'fact' against 'fiction' in this way unsettles notions of the security of past, present and future as distinct temporal regimes that are integral to the concept of linear progress. This action reminds us that we can never exhaust the potential of the present, that the future can never be finished and that the past is not behind us.

Tracing the affective ripples that connect Olive Morris, Sisters Uncut and the tenets of Marxism is not an attempt to identify straightforward continuities, rather it acknowledges how placing archival material in an aporetic temporality can distort historical time. By 'historical time' I refer to a temporality whose organisation is dependent on world historical events and in light of modernity has come to be fixed in a straightforward past-present-future-chronology that moves in one direction, most famously theorised by Koselleck. In her work, Victoria Browne (2014), attempts to reconceptualise historical time, making the case that it is polytemporal – a "lived time" which surely moves in more than one direction" (2014: 2). I break with this reconceptualisation, to argue that the notion of historical time is underpinned by a Hegelian teleological progression based on a colonial conception of 'World History' that must be abandoned entirely. In my analysis, the substance of History is not defined by a chronological temporality but rather by a temporality that oscillates, that is constantly on the move. It rejects the presentist thesis that all things are self-evident by attempting to enable temporal regimes to encroach on one another.

Constructing an aporetic temporality in which to place texts enables the tracing of connections to take place. I understand tracing as an affective technology which includes the use of speculation, fabulation, comparative visual and discourse analysis. This action helps elucidate flows, and non-linguistic intensities of feeling that connect these texts across time. Gregg and Seigworth (2010) argue that at its most anthropomorphic, affect theory relates to a "force" or forces of encounter. I am interested in the emotional aftermath of quotidian encounters with archival material, with the "accumulative *beside-ness*" (2010: 2) that affect theory intends to clarify. Ahmed (2010) writes that "affect is what sticks, what sustains and preserves the connection between ideas, values and objects" (2010: 29). Noting the strange lingerings of the 'past' in the 'present' and the role these lingerings play into the constitution of the future is pertinent in understanding where the desire to participate in material transformation emerges from. I understand archival material as part of a forcefield of relations, which have an impact on our understanding of the world, its limits and its possibilities. This forcefield of relations shapes our political will, as well as what is possible to conceive of for ourselves and others. In other words, the practice of identifying how Marxist thought seems to echo, reverberate and linger, of bringing Marx, Morris and Sisters Uncut into the same temporality and enabling them to face one another is connected to my contention that such a meeting has the power to cultivate the political desire to resist in myself as a researcher and in you, reader, for the purposes of sustaining grassroots movements.

The scope of my interest is the relationship between being *moved* by archival material and our desire, intention and capacity to materially resist violent conditions. I am interested in the rhythms, forces and modalities that come to define these encounters and how they warp temporality. In the space of my inquiry, I wish to imagine it were possible to rub Marx, Olive Morris and Sisters Uncut against one another, to loop them around each other affectively and theoretically. In order to avoid positioning Marxism as my theoretical starting point, tracing enables me to open up a hermeneutical window that understands radical theory as a thoroughly interdependent and circular endeavor. As theory informs praxis, so the past and future bleed into the present, eliminating the linearity inherent to notions of 'beginning' and 'end.'

Hall et al. (1978) noted that race and gender are modalities through which proletarian life is lived, experienced and resisted, this claim fortifies Marxist thought, rather than diminishes it. I also propose tracing as a method because it enables me to question how accusations of the diminishment of class analysis reify orthodox Marxism as the origin point of political thought, so that everyone who comes after Marx must answer him as their predecessor, rather than address him as a comrade with whom they share temporal space. Tracing helps break down the often staid and totalising logic that analyses of race, gender, sexuality and/or colonialism are somehow corrosive to Marxist epistemologies by opening space for dialogue, dissent, lingering and repetition. Political struggle does not begin with Marx, nor do contemporary social movements simply adopt Marxist principles in this thing called 'the present' which is distinct from 'the past' in which this thinking originates. The relationship between Marx, Olive Morris and Sisters Uncut is reciprocal, I wager that they can and do touch and rub up against one another outside of a linear temporal landscape and that thinking Marxism differently requires us to remain attentive to the hapticality that is produced as a result.

***

Rather than begin with Marx, let us begin in Lambeth Archives in South London. Under the careful watch of archivists who remind me that the presence of pens, food and drinks are prohibited when handling the material, I come across an essay written by Olive Morris in February 1978, presumably for her undergraduate degree in Politics at Manchester University.

Figure 2: Olive Morris essay, February 1978[4]

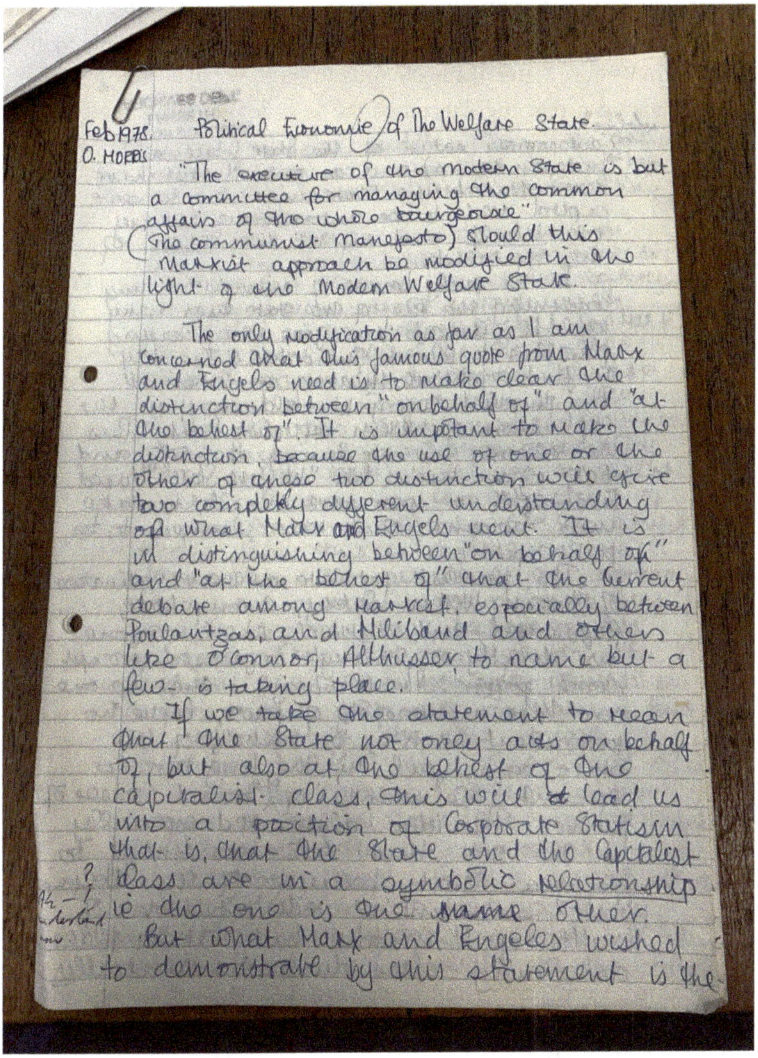

Feb 1978.
O. MORRIS

Political Economie of The Welfare State.

"The executive of the modern State is but a committee for managing the common affairs of the whole bourgeoisie" (The communist Manefesto) Should this Marxist approach be modified in the light of the Modern Welfare State.

The only modification as far as I am concerned that this famous quote from Marx and Engels need is to make clear the distinction between "on behalf of" and "at the behest of". It is important to make the distinction, because the use of one or the other of these two distinction will give two completely different understanding of what Marx and Engels meant. It is in distinguishing between "on behalf of" and "at the behest of" that the current debate among Marxist, especially between Poulantzas, and Miliband and others like O'connor, Althusser, to name but a few - is taking place.

If we take the statement to mean that the State not only acts on behalf of, but also at the behest of the capitalist class, this will lead us into a position of Corporate Statism that is, that the State and the Capitalist class are in a symbolic relationship ie the one is the same other.

But what Marx and Engeles wished to demonstrate by this statement is the

---

4 This image was reproduced by kind permission of London Borough of Lambeth, Archives Department.

In this essay, she attempts to answer the question: "The executive of the modern state is a committee for managing the common affairs of the bourgeoisie." (The Communist Manifesto) Should this Marxist approach be modified in light of the Modern Welfare State?" (Lambeth Archives, n.p., 2009)

Morris argues that the illusion of the so-called welfare state does not obscure the state's original function as a protector of private property or a guardian for the accumulation of capital.

> The question then is how does Marxism explain the undisputable changes which have taken place in capitalist society, changes brought about through such channels as the welfare state? For Marx and the Marxist alike, the role of the state is primarily to protect private property and in protecting it, the state also has to legitimise the existence of this backboard ownership. Especially if (the state) continues to assist capital in enduring the extraction of surplus value from the majority for the benefit of the few – this is capitalism's main contradiction. (Lambeth, n.p., Archives, 2009)

In her analysis, the Keynesian welfare state is an ideologically harmonizing move from the bourgeoisie that makes piecemeal concessions to citizens whilst maintaining the fundamentally extractive and dispossessive nature of capitalism. Morris notes how the Welfare State is dependent on the exploited labour of workers from the former colonies. In line with social reproductionists, she also notes how women's care work within homes and state institutions such as hospitals and schools are crucial not only in the creation of workers but the maintenance of the state's ideological harmonizing mission. The implication of her analysis is that the state remains an obstructive force in the lives of workers and that material transformation might only occur when it is displaced via a proletarian revolution. Morris recognises the role of the state as the arbiter between classes and indicates that the destruction of this relationship is a necessity.

Following Morris, Marx and Engels similarly outlined the necessity of workers' antagonistic relationship to the state under capitalism. In *Anti-Duhring: Herr Eugen Duhring's Revolution in Science* (1987) Engels writes,

> The proletariat seizes from state power and turns the means of production into state property to begin with. But thereby it abolishes itself as the proletariat, abolishes all class distinctions and class antagonisms, and also abolishes the state as state. (1987: 267)

With Morris, they point toward the necessity of seizing state power in order to bring about truly transformative political conditions for workers. Marx's reflections on the efforts of the Paris Commune are also pertinent here. In the preface of the 1872 edition of *The Communist Manifesto*, updated in light of the events at the Paris Commune, Marx and Engels remark that "the working class cannot simply lay hold of the ready-made state machinery and wield it for its own purposes." (2012: 103). Indeed, they implore their audience to understand that as-is, the state cannot be wielded on its own terms, its purpose must be first reconfigured. Marx and Engels argue that the culmination of class struggle is a dictatorship of the proletariat, which necessitates a withering away of the state as we know it. This withering away occurs in the proletarian command of the organisational aspects of the state, which is only a temporary stage in the movement towards a classless society. To perform an analysis that traces, is to note how the demand for the withering away of the state appears in both texts under different guises. If we attune our ears, we might hear the echoes of political desire embedded in analysis. Morris follows Marx and Engels by arguing that the Welfare State is simply a smokescreen which obscures the necessity of the state's destruction and then speaks back to them by incorporating an analysis of the exploitation of workers from former colonies in the maintenance of the British state, an undeveloped notion in Marx's political writing. Marx and Engels offer Morris a framework that enables her to further elucidate the intricacies of her material conditions as a black worker who is subject to oppressive conditions constituted and exacerbated by her racialisation and gendering. They pass ideas back and forth. By refusing to understand these texts using prevailing temporal logics, the two thinkers begin an exchange that builds:

*For Marx and the Marxist alike, the role of the state is primarily to protect private property. The proletariat seizes from state power and turns the means of production into state property to begin with. **Especially if (the state) continues to assist capital in enduring the extraction of surplus value.***"

The above is merely a textual representation of this exchange, but placing the texts inside of an aporetic temporality creates a new theoretical conjuncture in which the tenets of Marxism, expressed across the temporal divide coalesce, to form a different political and artistic imperative. This textual collaboration creates an affective resonance which indicates that resistant forces, though separated by temporal divides, are co-constitutive, made up of one another.

Morris' organising and determination to forge transnational links between radical struggles might also be read as a form of radical reciprocity with Marx. Coincidentally, I come across multiple photographs of her as a member of the student delegation of the Society for Anglo-Chinese Understanding who visited China in 1977 in order to understand how communism had been built and sustained. In an article she wrote for *SPEAK OUT!*, the Brixton Black Women's Group newsletter, Olive examines the function of the Republic and the possibility of transforming conditions for the proletariat.

> After the People's Republic was founded in 1949, the peasants were freed from exploitation of big landlords and a system of collective production began which over the years has gone through many stages. Today it takes the form of the People's Commune which combines all social activities. It organizes the running of small factories, schools, medical teams, clinics, cultural activities and of course, agriculture. The People's Commune has furthered the people's confidence in dealing with the job of planting, protecting and harvesting crops, guaranteeing food for the mass of Chinese people all year round. (Lambeth Archives, 2009)

The desire for the destruction of the capitalist state expressed in Morris' essays exists not merely as Marxism's successor but also as its companion. This political demand is testament to how Marxist principles might be echoed, remade, rearticulated and accumulate beside across the many years that separate Olive Morris from Marx and Engels. They neither eclipse nor are eclipsed by each other, rather in tracing the echoes that emanate from her work, Olive helps rescue Marxism from the tomb of the past, held together by linear historicity, by rearticulating a desire for the death of the state that was also expressed by her 'predecessors.' Morris revives Marx to accompany her; perhaps they speak in one voice, at different tones and registers, to say: **The withering away of the capitalist state is a necessity.** To return to the work of Victoria Browne (2013), Morris' contributions are part of a temporal loop, a Kierkegaardian mode of "recollecting forward" which can be understood as "a kind of echoing which does not passively repeat but actively transforms past and present simultaneously" (Jones 2009: 13). Political will scatters itself across temporal zones. Repetition, echoes, resurfacings occur because conferred authority of "History" has been displaced by an aporetic temporality. Morris' relationship to Marx can be distilled here precisely because another understanding of temporality enables us to recognise that they both write across History, driven by the fact that the contest over power between the proletariat and the bourgeoisie has not yet been resolved. The desire for the state to wither contained in these archival documents emanates through an affective charge, reaches us in the here and now and strengthens our own imperative to resist as thinkers, readers and those invested in class struggle.

***

An organiser holds a banner outside of the courtroom. **MET POLICE: BLOOD ON YOUR HANDS** is messaging in line with Sisters Uncut's history of evocative imagery and rhetoric; it provides a direct critique of the carcerality of state power. The statement urges the public to reject the explanation by the MET Police communications office that the sitting police officer who murdered Sarah Everard in 2021 was an aberration, 'a lone officer' who was not representative of the police's function in society as whole. In light of the deaths and/or brutality inflicted on Cherry Groce, Bibaa Henry and Nicole Smallman, Joy Gardner, Annabella Landsberg, Sarah Reed, Sarah Everard and many more, Sisters Uncut demand the wholesale withdrawal of consent to be policed. BECOME UNGOVERNABLE, they chant. In opposition to the Police, Crime, Sentencing and Courts Act (2022) making its way through Parliament at the same time, they organise counter protests, cop-watch groups and set off hundreds of rape alarms outside White Chapel police station. They put forward an abolitionist vision for navigating carceral landscapes: **the police do not protect us, always and forever, we keep each other safe.**

Building on the work of Marx, Lenin writes: *A standing army and police are the chief instruments of state power. But how can it be otherwise?* (2020:11) The purpose of reading this image alongside Lenin's interpretation of Marxism and Olive Morris's theoretical contribution is to underscore how the image orientates us towards that 'otherwise.' I read the image in question both as evidence of a political form of direct-action and as a form of enlivening cultural production. I understand the banner and the demand it displays to be part of a set of visual and aesthetic choices intended to denaturalise a police state. The image captures the moment that the cultural work comes into contact with the public. In this moment, there is a communication of political desire that mirrors and echoes Lenin and Morris. *But how can it be otherwise?* The image is an invitation for the onlooker to expand their own imaginative capacity.

If the state is propped up by police power (Lenin), we must remain aware of the illusion of the welfare state (Morris) and its withering is dependent on a dictatorship of the proletariat (Engels), then contemporary calls for the abolition of policing represent an extension of the Marxist demand for the cultivation of working class power. **MET POLICE, BLOOD ON YOUR HANDS** might also be read as a call for the reconfiguration of the state, its seizure by the proletariat pending its dissolution.

In *Feminism Interrupted; Disrupting Power* (2020), I analysed the danger of liberalism's insistence on policing as a public good for the safety of women. The use of forms of direct action by feminist resistance groups such as Sisters Uncut illustrate how the cultivation of working class power is directly connected to and powered by the delegitimisation of policing through a critical analysis of its function as a mechanism of the state:

> In the liberal feminist rationale, the police and prisons are necessary because they protect women from danger. They are necessary because without them, society would descend into chaos… but the police are deployed to do the state's bidding and are enmeshed in the oppressive consequences of this task. This is why, despite liberal feminism's insistence, increased numbers of women entering the police force can never transform its practice. State killings act as another mechanism to remove women from public life. (Olufemi 2020: 31)

I include this analysis with the aim of highlighting how the cultural object (in this instance, an image) provides visual representation of the groups recognition of the state's obsolescence, it is another avenue for the consideration of similar desires across temporal locations. Following Morris' elucidation of capitalist contradiction; reading the texts against one another propels us towards an analysis that understands how even the seemingly benevolent state, propped up by general anxieties about violence, is dangerous. The demand in the image implicitly instructs its audience to want more, it builds the desirous ground from which Marxist analysis proceeds by naming the violence of the state's institutions – and consolidating this claim with actions, mobilisations and skill-sharing that enable its audience to resist its hegemony in the present moment. The political imperative to transform the state as we know it is not displaced into a future that is won by virtue of obedience to a stadial historicism but rather found, rehearsed and enacted by way of temporal experimentation in the present moment.

If the image captures the "moment" that the political demand enters public space, Morris' archival essay is private evidence of the consolidation of a political standpoint, the texts produced by Marx, Engels and Lenin offer an enduring lens through which to read and rethink how capitalist domination expresses itself. When made to exist in the same temporality, the affective pull of these objects consolidates liberatory promise; they shore up prepersonal, non-conscious intensities that consolidate one another, producing an affinity and attachment to freedom as a realisable phenomena. If, as Ruth Wilson Gilmore (2017: 226) argues, freedom is a place – then the affective phenomena produced by experimentation with cultural material orientates us all in the direction of that place and asks us to locate it.

***

I want to end with a recognition that my attempt to trace affective echoes and the desires they produce, my brief experiment in recording what repeats, is not intended to fix that echo or repetition in place. I understand desire using Berlant's definition of it as 'a state of attachment and the cloud of possibility that is generated by the gap between an object's specificity and the needs and promises projected onto it.' In this instance, the question is not if the object's specificity (the withering away of the state) is *obtainable* but how the cultural objects that come under my analysis becomes a receptacle for revolutionary needs and promises that are projected on to it. When I identify echoes, I am not arguing that Marx, Morris and Sisters Uncut share an unbroken vision or set of demands without dissent or disruption. I am suggesting that placing them in a different temporal space illuminates the way their approaches hold, speak back, enrich and contour one another and in turn can produce an affective orientation that reignites our desire to resist via material struggle.

These subjects relate *in spite* of their different temporal locations. Across action and text, in letters, essays and visual material – all three subjects express a desire for the state as we know it to give way, to wither and slowly die. The existence of the demands in this ephemera makes the possibility of enacting the state's disappearance tangible for their relative audiences and those who engage with their work across temporal divides. Thinking Marxism differently means embracing the role of ephemeral and creative methods in relation to Marxist critique; thinking with and against History – in order for this tension to extend forms of Marxist analysis related to the operation of the base and superstructure, the form of revolution, the historical development of capital and the nature of class struggle. What lingers in Morris and Sisters Uncut affirms and extends the ground on which Marxism is built. Their words and actions put Marx to *good use*, sending reverberations that meet his words in 1852 and leave remnants of the future in it.

References

Ahmed, Sara (2010): "Happy Objects." In: Melissa Gregg/Gregory J. Seigworth (eds.), The Affect Theory Reader, Durham and London: Duke University Press, pp. 29–51.

Beiner, Ronald (1984): "Walter Benjamin's Philosophy of History." In: Political Theory 12/3, pp. 423–434 (http://www.jstor.org/stable/191516).

Bradley, Rizvana (2015): "Reinventing Capacity: Black Femininity's Lyrical Surplus and the Cinematic Limits of 12 Years a Slave." In: Black Camera 7/1, pp. 162–178.

Browne, Victoria (2013): "Backlash, Repetition, Untimeliness: The Temporal Dynamics of Feminist Politics." In: Hypatia 28/4, pp. 905–920.

Browne, Victoria (2014): Feminism, Time, and Nonlinear History, New York: Palgrave Macmillan US.

Gregg, Melissa/Seigworth. Gregory J eds. (2010): "An Inventory of Shimmers." In: Melissa Gregg/Gregory J. Seigworth (eds.), The Affect Theory Reader, Durham and London: Duke University Press, pp. 1–4.

Hall, Stuart/Critcher, Chas/Jefferson, Tony/Clarke, John/Roberts, Brian (1978): Policing the Crisis: Mugging, the State and Law and Order, London: Macmillan.

Jones, Rachel (2009): "Between Fractures and Folds: Battersby on Active Matter" and 'Others Within.'" (Unpublished manuscript presented at Situated Selves conference at the University of Liverpool).

Kelley, Robin (2008): Freedom Dreams: The Black Radical Imagination, Boston: Beacon Press.

Lenin, Vladimir (2020): The State and Revolution, Paris: Foreign Languages Press.

Marx, Karl (1975 [1852]): "Marx to Weydemeyer Dated March 5, 1852." In: Karl Marx/Friedrich Engels (eds.), Selected Correspondence, Moscow: Progress Publishers, p. 669.

Marx, Karl/Engels, Friedrich (1987): Collected Works Volume 25: Frederick Engels: Anti-Dühring. Dialectics of Nature, New York: International Publishers.

Marx, Karl/Engels, Friedrich (1975): Selected Correspondence, Moscow: Progress Publishers.
Marx, Karl/Engels, Friedrich (1992): The Communist Manifesto. New York: Oxford University Press.
Marx, Karl/Engels, Friedrich (2012): "Preface to the German Edition of 1872." In: Jeffrey C. Isaac (eds.), The Communist Manifesto, New Haven and London: Yale University Press.
Olufemi, Lola (2020): Feminism Interrupted, London: Pluto Press.
Olufemi, Lola (2021): Experiments in Imagining Otherwise, London: Hajar Press, pp. 22–23.
Sisters Uncut (2021): "Sisters Uncut: 'Why We're Launching National Intervention Training after Sarah Everard's Kidnap by Cop", September 30, 2021 (https://gal-dem.com/wayne-couzens-arrested-sarah-intervention/).
Wilkie, Alex/Savransky, Martin/Rosengarten, Marsha (eds.) (2017): Speculative Research: The Lure of Possible Futures, Abingdon: Routledge.
Wilson Gilmore, Ruth (2017): "Abolition Geography and the Problem of Innocence." In: Gaye Theresa Johnson/Alex Lubin (eds.), Futures of Black Radicalism, London: Verso, pp. 224–241.

Archives

Lambeth Archives, IV/279/1/11/1-30. 2009. Olive Morris Collection. Essays.

Inverting Marxism[1]

Jules Joanne Gleeson

This essay will return to the themes introduced in the 2021 collection *Transgender Marxism*[2]. Either one of these words can draw a strong (and divisive reaction). Why bring these two concerns together?

Our collection yoked a focus on a stigmatised minority, and the global majority (those left 'doubly free', having been stripped from control over the means of production.) This bracketing clearly caused some consternation among parts of the left. There are those who assert that Marxism's materialism is counterposed with concern for transgender people, and especially that it militates against prioritisation of identities.

Trans struggles are not alone in facing down this reflex of attempted relegation. As explored by Michael Richmond and Alex Charnley's newly published *Fractured: Race, Class, Gender and the Hatred of Identity Politics* (2022), an attempt to divorce class politics and liberatory understandings of minorities has become entrenched. By marked contrast, twinning gender deviance and class war is quite intuitive as a set of associations for the global right. From media figureheads like Tucker Carlson to thriving syncretist political movements in Hungary, Brazil and Britain, contemporary nationalists have proven fully prepared to confront challenges to workplace exploitation and fraying household norms in one moment. In this sense *Transgender Marxism* provided a sort of catch-up to the determined attempts of fascists to smash contemporary threats to both Capital and the private households that churn out its workforces – moves

---

1 This article was originally presented at the workshop "Confronting the Specters of Marxism. Analysing New Currents in Intersectional, Feminist, Queer, and Transgender Marxism in Times of Multiples Crisis" held on October 13–14, 2022, at the University of Bielefeld. It is being reproduced with the author's permission and remains unchanged in format and content since its initial presentation.
2 See: Gleeson, Jules Joanne/O'Rourke, Elle (eds.) (2021): Transgender Marxism, London: Pluto Press (https://www.plutobooks.com/9780745341668/transgender-marxism/).

which leftists have too often been slow, tame and unimaginative in their responses to.

Our approach with the collection was to anthologise a set of commissioned essays from those we'd already seen develop transgender theorising through one historical materialist tradition or another. The result was a collection that drew not only on appeals to political economy but methods from psychoanalysis to phenomenology (transition as experienced) to epistemological explorations. To be schematic, there are three entry points to grasping the struggle *Transgender Marxism* addresses:

- The Workplace
- The Household
- The Clinic

Let's enter the workplace via a June 2022 report from the Washington Post (hardly a radical outlet) titled "A trans 24-year-old finds his voice and ignites a union effort at his Starbucks." (Tan 2022). Reporting based on interviews with one unionising Starbucks worker, Ian Miller, the piece recounts both Miller's transition, and successful unionise in his franchised workplace.

The US chain of the global coffee store chain Starbucks had offered trans employees coverage for healthcare (HRT and surgeries), drawing into their workforce a substantial number of retail worker proletarians otherwise unlikely to have steady access to essential care. Yet as the (inevitable) intensification of exploitation through precarious work contracts came to bite Starbucks' workforces as a whole, this same conditional privileging was swiftly redeployed as more or less explicit leverage by corporate management: resistance to management meant risking *de facto* medical detransition. What had been a worker privilege became (under tension) a tool to attempt disruption of proletarian autonomy.

Reading this reporting for the first time, it was hard not to see the reporting as an inadvertent gloss of the arguments advanced in *Transgender Marxism* (especially the chapters of Michelle O'Brien, and Kade Doyle Griffiths.) Namely that attempting to grasp transition in *opposition to* or *hierarchical prioritisation* against class politics will lead to a weaker understanding of both sexed identifications and class struggles, as they unfold this century. From retail to sex work, specific labouring conditions have drawn in disproportionately trans workforces to conditions both disagreeable to unionisation, and quickly reshaped by the influx of particularly stigmatised workers predisposed toward militant conclusions.

Yet despite this particular risk, trans (and other LGBT) workers were clearly at the forefront of the Starbucks labour organising, introducing unions to workplaces in a series of breakthroughs reminiscent of the recent drives through Big Tech firms such as Google and Amazon (in that they targeted workplaces clearly built around the presupposition that organised labour politics was not a concern.)

It also demonstrates that inclusion of LGBT matters in frameworks of "Corporate Social Responsibility" has resulted in genuine opportunities for contemporary struggle, however craven and opportunistic these deployments have been. Widespread transphobia had previously ensured a sharper demarcation between so-called "skilled" labourers (especially in tech) and the broader population denied working opportunities through hostility from employers. While much of the "pro-LGBT" glossing of major corporations had gone little deeper than draping their social media accounts with flag avatars for one month a year, cases such as Starbucks shows the prospects (and the limits!) for a more profound transformation of conditions in capitalist exploitation.

In this conditional provision of otherwise unaffordable procedures, Starbucks are exemplary in mobilising the 'perk' of relative proletarian privileges, providing healthcare to their workforce with both a lure to attract workers otherwise without assurances that their specific health needs will be met, and a disciplining instrument that through this very extension of transition provisioning tethers each trans worker to their continued employment.

The obvious *failure* of this to stabilise the union free working conditions which prevailed since the company's foundation should give us hope. For Marxists, this sketch of personal development blossoming to workplace struggle is probably the most comforting, and easily integrated face of *Transgender Marxism*.

Secondly, we start where struggles with transitions are often taken to begin: **The household**.

To begin by stating the obvious: none of us can avoid implication or involvement when talking of normative upbringings! But more specifically trans experiences are set through and against the private household as a commonplace site for developmental violence and dispossession (or the pointed threat of it). While far from uniform, an overall picture of what it means to be confined in (or to escape) the closet can hardly begin without bringing private households into critical view.

While the division between the 'properly political' and private affairs has been problematised by any number of thinkers, work bridging this schism still feels counter-intuitive to many. It has to be said that Marxism as a school of thought has often attracted those who long for a grandiose "modal" overview, to better allow for a remove from the mess and intimacy found in questions around upbringing. From this elevated point of view, whatever aspiration, idiosyncracy or prejudice was baked into us through our household of origin finds some ultimate direction in the pulsations of accumulation, or valorization.

But in recent years Marxist Feminism has generated a substantial body of work which intends to bring labour power's continuous generation into clearer view, exactly through a collapsing of any loosely imagined partitioned between worker identity, and rearing. Those developing this perspective include Cinzia Arruzza ("Remarks on Gender", *Viewpoint Magazine* 2014), Holly Lewis (*The Politics of Everybody: Feminism, Queer Theory, and Marxism at the Intersection*, 2016), Tithi Bhattacharya (*Social Reproducing: Remapping Class, Recentering Oppression* 2017) and Aaron Jaffe (*Social Reproduction and the Socialist Horizon*, 2020).

While Marx uses the word 'reproduction' in a very polyvalent way throughout *Capital*, this vein of theory has focused primarily on the way that capitalist workforces are obliged to be *self-constituting*, in order for exploitation to continue. In other words the lengthy and arduous processes that go into 'showing up ready to work' before each clock-in, or billable hour.

The challenge posed by these thinkers to existing Marxist social theory is exactly that a rigorous accounting of workforces must extend beyond the workplace (at least as conventionally understood). This theoretical demand was backed by an upsurge of militant struggle which merger worker concerns and struggles typically classed as "women's liberation", such as abortion rights and femicide.

While several contributions to *Transgender Marxism* were fully or primarily informed by this Social Reproduction tendency in Marxist Feminism, our editorial work especially was closely informed by the work of Angela Mitropoulos into histories of *oikomia*, or household management. Mitropoulos' work places into a longer context the incessant references to familial authority which pepper the thinking of right wing demagogues, drawing attention to the same concern in pre-modern thinkers such as Xenophon. Drawing from this schema, we find that private households do not only play a disciplining role for the individual workers reared by them, but continue a legacy of ruling class household management that we might rank alongside "statesmanship". As well as providing the continuous churn of fresh workforces required by Capital, private households equally perpetuate a process of normative establishment that long predates modernity. These historic variations in what Arruzza terms 'patriarchal relations' (in favour of a conceptually autonomous/systemic Patriarchy).

From this view we can come to see more clearly why the global right have come so intuitively to see trans lives as a threat to "the family". The cries of Q-Anon conspiracists to "Save the children!" do not appear because they truly consider childhood sacred, but as a rearguard defence of a fraying project instituted by the New Right. In their attempt to delimit acceptable contours of the human these reactionaries are drawing from a deep wellspring: Aristotle classed as monstrous offspring which bore qualitatively little resemblance to their parents.

Finally, we turn to **the clinic** as a site of struggle and the entangled role of clinicians in identity discipline.

But no account of clinical politics today could begin without the campaign of "stochastic terror" which now dominates the United States, with doctors alongside professionals from librarians to teachers who find themselves hounded by loosely organised mobs targeting online distributed targets lists of those deemed too LGBT, and smeared as "groomers".

Since our book's publication we've witnessed a stark intensification of militant transphobic politics oriented towards clinical care providers. This takes the form both of legislatures attempting to institute "model bills" outlawing healthcare for trans youth, and agitation that takes a more direct approach to menacing queers out of public life, and professionals out of providing us services. In the United States both new media provocateurs with enormous online fanbases, and more conventional media outlets such as Fox News have repeatedly targeted the ire of their movement onto clinics (including children's hospitals) which offer services to trans patients. Their coverage has reproduced their material with glosses that accuse physicians of "mutilation" and "child abuse", posting their faces and contact details and urging followers to pursue them. Similarly, groups such as the Proud Boys have stormed libraries hosting drag events.

The purpose of this continuously generated outrage is a strategy of terrorism drawn from the pro-life movement (which various key figures overlap with). Their aim is to steadily reduce provision of trans healthcare across "Red States" through raising the stakes for any professionals considering offering these services, through the same violent means that abortion clinics were shuttered years prior to the recent overturning of federal protection of abortion rights (Roe vs. Wade) through a Supreme Court reversal.

Meanwhile, liberal defences of these services have usually failed to reckon with the reality that this debate is focused only on the minority of trans children with fully supportive parents. Defences of this kind have typically run that it is the rightful place for parents and professional healthcare providers to decide the best course, disregarding the widespread reality of youth homelessness that remains the reality for such a high proportion of non-conforming youth. Liberalism can offer only a vision of benign drift toward a reformed future.

Having begun with the moves the US right has taken against clinicians, the oppositional tone taken by *Transgender Marxism* towards clinicians may require some explanation. Thankfully, the Marxist tradition is perfectly placed to appreciate disputes among the ruling class, including their most violent and seemingly antithetical appearance.

Recently, it's become unfashionable to juxtapose the influence of Michel Foucault and Karl Marx (especially after the revisionist theoretical and historical work of the late Christopher Chitty). However it must be admitted that those following Foucault's legacy in earnest (or at least as earnestly as his infamous ironising allows...) have made great headway in "deneutralising" clinical practice, and uncovering the pervasive reach of clinical categorisation into unexamined understandings. There's a lot more to be said here about the breakthroughs and limits of critical histories (in short, they've been rich in concrete insights for the inner workings of particular capitalist institutions, while sometimes winnowed in their comparative scope.)

But primarily the work I've encouraged and edited stresses is the often understated *labour* at work on the other side of the clinical relation. A significant number of trans people are immersed in guiding others through clinical contexts, and in places supplanting their typical roles. These informal community workforces operate through methods and venues that are weakly understood by those not directly requiring them, forming a sort of ersatz civil society. From distribution of key knowledge through relevant circles, to clandestine deprofessionalised development of skillsets those formally expected to deliver services can too often not be relied to perform, it's this activity which forms the basis for the 'insurrectionary' moments Foucault's method are minded towards documenting.

While personally I had previously approached this more strictly in terms of "social reproduction", the same concern is approached by thinkers deploying various vocabularies throughout *Transgender Marxism*. However we refer to them, community labours must be understood to grasp why it is "the transgender question" has come to be posed so frequently today.

***

The event this essay was prepared for addressed the 'Spectres of Marx' haunting the academy. But is the type of social thought under discussion primarily a concern for academics? I'm not convinced.

While there were a handful of university lecturers included in *Transgender Marxism* (two still active by my count), the only tenured professor was Jordy Rosenberg (who provided an afterword.) By and large the insights documented in *Transgender Marxism* are "academic" only insofar as they were developed by those burning out of that context, if indeed they ever had access to such credential-minded institutions at all. So we need to question how far any "return of Marx" to the academy is truly necessary for the further fruitful development of social revolutionary thinking.

I don't want to provide any oversimplified answer to that question, having posed it. Today's relations between academic Marxism and thinking focused elsewhere defy easy characterisation, and certainly we should avoid any dichotomising view between "NEET thought" and those with scholarly dayjobs. Especially, I would like to highlight the role played by online fanbases and social media participation in developing the reception of Marxists who have not enjoyed fulsome institutional prominence. Consider for example the recent hubbub around Michael Heinrich and Jairus Banaji, neither of whom can be said to have enjoyed conventional (that is, managerial) success as academics would view it, yet have attracted enthused followings animating topics often taken to be dry and abstruse (Marxology and agrarian labour in pre-industrial political economies).

Beyond this interplay of scholarly publishing and its online enthusiasts, intellectual activity twinning trans and queer critique with Marxist theory is often concentrated in dedicated journals, zines and movement publications. As a case in point, the title of this talk is "Inverting Marxism", a homage to the intermittent transfeminist materialist journal *Invert*. Named after the sexological category of "inversion" (most famously associated with Havelock Ellis), today usually taken to be an outmoded and effeminacy-centred framework for understanding homo/transsexuality. Chairing their panel at *Historical Materialism* Conference 2019, I was confronted with the realisation that a profound development of concerns familiar to me that had run parallel to the work I'd fostered more directly. Years later the influence of this current was also apparent in an essay by Sandow Sinai "On Returning Things To Their Proper Places"[3], where Naomi Alizah Cohen's reading of Moshe Postone surfaced to address the entrenchment of anti-semitism alongside anti-identitarianism in the contemporary left.

Along with their more gay communism oriented counterparts *Pinko* and *Homintern*, a lively circuit twinning Marxism and sex (or sexuality) seemed to be forming by the later 2010s. Notably though each of these publications proved short lived and prone to hiatus, and have proven rather less durable than dedicated Marxist theory publications outside the academy – such as *Viewpoint Mag*, *Salvage* or *Spectre Journal*. This ephemerality was something we hoped to avoid with our anthologising work, but seems set to return as a cycle of flourishing and dissolution given the unsteady resources available for instantiating communist thought in lasting forums.

So I close by introducing *Invert* to highlight that despite *Transgender Marxism*'s voluminous character (around 300 pages), no single publication could hope to encompass the intellectual activity which currently surrounds questions of transition and class struggle. Beyond the seventeen or so contributors we brought together, theorists such as Treva Ellison, Bini Adamczak, Alex Adamson and Kay Gabriel have provided approaches spanning a wide range of disciplines to address questions which have yet to be settled through revolution. Hopefully following *Transgender Marxism* the auxiliary work of social theorisation can continue apace, with new coalitions and fresh cravings coming messily into view.

---

3   See: Sinai, Sandow (2022): "On Returning Things to Their Proper Places." In: Hypocrite Reader 99, (http://hypocritereader.com/99/proper-places).

References

Arruzza, Cinzia (2014): "Remarks on Gender." In: Viewpoint Magazine 4 (https://viewpointmag.com/2014/09/02/remarks-on-gender/).

Bhattacharya, Tithi (2017): Social Reproducing: Remapping Class, Recentering Oppression, London: Pluto Press.

Gleeson, Jules Joanne/O'Rourke, Elle (eds.) (2021): Transgender Marxism, London: Pluto Press.

Jaffe, Aaron (2020): Social Reproduction and the Socialist Horizon, London: Pluto Press.

Lewis, Holly (2016): The Politics of Everybody: Feminism, Queer Theory, and Marxism at the Intersection. London: Zed Books.

Sinai, Sandow (2022): "On Returning Things to Their Proper Places." In: Hypocrite Reader 99, (http://hypocritereader.com/99/proper-places).

Tan, Rebecca (2022): "A trans 24-year-old finds his voice and ignites a union effort at his Starbucks", June 22, 2022 (https://www.washingtonpost.com/dc-md-va/2022/06/21/starbucks-union-workers-trans-lgbtq/).

Rethinking Marx with(in) Latin American Societies. A Conversation with Verónica Gago

Edith Otero Quezada[1]

Rethinking Marx's *oeuvre* requires not only to look at the various interpretations that have emerged over time, but also to reinterpret it from historically specific local and global perspectives. The present interview with *Ni Una Menos* activist and intellectual Verónica Gago will do so for the Latin American context. In the region, there have been numerous attempts to address and recontextualise the philosopher's legacy, from José Carlos Mariátegui's work on issues of land and the indigenous as a political subject to José Aricó's complex labour of Marxian translation (and political reinterpretation). The endeavours of Lohana Berkins, a communist transvestite, in popular education and cooperatives have also been crucial for understanding the interconnections between transvestism, transfeminisms, and class struggle in Argentina. Lastly, reflections from feminist Marxism or feminist materialism are essential, with figures like Luisina Bolla, Natalia Romé, Luci Cavallero, and, in the specific context of this dialogue, the militant research of Verónica Gago.

How can we rediscover Marx without falling into reductions? How can we give space to diverse subjects and political bodies? Is there room for new internationalisms? How can we overcome the division between theory and political practice? These and other questions were the initial driving force of this conversation. I thank Verónica Gago for the opportunity for this enriching exchange. It challenges us and invites us to think about the dynamics of contemporary capitalism from Marx and beyond.

In her works *Neoliberalism from Below* (2017), *Feminist International* (2020), and, co-authored by Luci Cavallero, *A Feminist Reading of Debt* (2021), we find a complex and innovative framework of philosophical schools – post-structuralist, Marxist, Latin American, decolonial, feminist – which in turn intersects

---

1 Translation from Spanish by Edith Otero Quezada.

with her feminist militancy in *Ni Una Menos* in Argentina. In her analyses, we witness an Argentina criss-crossed by a multiple and expansive cartography of conflicts and resistances, with the feminist strike as a form of political practice that connects identity and class politics, manifesting itself against the financial violence of debt and building *feminist potencia* from diverse Body-Territories.

Throughout these pages, we discuss these issues and more with Verónica. Finally, I invite the reader to understand this exchange not as totalitarian analytical closures, but as entry points to begin other collective debates beyond the confines of academia and this book.

***

In your work, you have addressed a wide range of topics, including what you call "Expanded Extractivism," neoliberalism from below, and, more recently, new dynamics of debt. How do you apply a Marxist perspective in your work, especially in the context of Latin American societies? How does this perspective engage with others, such as decolonial and intersectional perspectives?

I read Marx, both at the public university and in different political education groups, the way he is often read: in fragments, repetitively, and generally through the lenses of different authors who interpret and discuss him, and, I believe, from whom we learn to read him. In this sense, it is a partial reading, always defined by our concerns at the times and the questions that arise in the struggles in which we are involved. A first landmark for me was reading him in relation to his "disencounter" with Latin America, to quote José Aricó, a great Argentine intellectual, translator, and editor whose work is fundamental. Through his writings, his biography as a militant activist, exile, and intellectual, I found a *thread* and a way of reading Marx that was very important. In his book *Marx y América Latina* (1982) [in English, *Marx and Latin America*], Aricó wonders how Marx's analysis of non-Western reality led him to his propositions and his contempt for Latin America. His "misreading" is interesting because Marx – as Aricó hypothesises – opens up a whole series of misreadings, to the point that in Latin America, Marxism came to be defined as "a grammatical expression of a very real historical challenge." A mistaken grammar, that of Marxism with Latin America, that attributed – to this continent – predicates that did not name it – whether due to the rigidity of nonexistent subjects, or the stubbornness of certain conditions that were never fulfilled. Rather than resorting to the familiar and readily available label of Eurocentrism, Aricó attempts to reconstruct – from within Marx's own thought – the conditions under which he considered colonial realities, in particular from his "strategic shift" after analysing the Irish situation. Especially because Aricó wants to demonstrate – and this is another one of the originalities of his research – that the image of Marx's eurocentrism is the product of the "official" version of the "Marxist *intelligentsia*," which marginalised Marx's texts on Spain, Russia, or Ireland as merely "circumstantial" writings. But even with Marx removed from eurocentrism, Latin America does not seem to interest him. Aricó transforms this contempt into a political tension. He contends that it is the identification of Latin American processes with European Bonapartism, as embodied in Simón Bolívar, and the legacy of Hegel's notion of "peoples without history" that hinders Marx's ability to understand Latin America. Because if Marx was able to grasp and value independent national realities, it was only because he was able to verify that "the people in struggle is *vital*." And to Marx, Latin America, which was considered an *empty* territory, held no such significance. Latin America, a place without *depth* in Marx's eyes, does not seem to have the real *foundation* of social struggles in order to become a nation. For Aricó, Marx makes an unexpected retreat to Hegel to describe something he fails to understand, even when this understanding was utterly shaken by the emergence of other, peripheral, different realities. Marx was unable to understand the singularity of Latin America because he did not envision an active popular will there, but rather a ruling class seeking to identify the nation with the state. So, to Marx's Hegelian view of Latin America as a place that lacks the determinations that might bring about a national struggle, Aricó adds Marx's anti-Hegelianism: the refusal to recognise a state's "potential to 'produce' a civil society." Marx cannot possibly concede that the state has its own effectiveness, says Aricó, without breaking its system. Aricó's thesis, then, shifts the label of eurocentrism to conclude that it is the "essentially statist" or "top-down" construction of Latin American nations that politically obscured Marx's understanding of the continent's singularity. And this is his blind spot: He supplants the "real movement" of Latin American social forces with the figure of Bolívar, while not acknowledging any "autonomy of the political" in the essentially state-based character of its national formations, which from the Marxist perspective, appears as a regression. However, Aricó says, that privilege of strictly political situations appears in Marx's "vanishing point," or more precisely, outside of his system. It is with this genealogical reconstruction of Marx's thought that Aricó's philosophical research explains the *mutual repulsion* between Marxism and Latin America that begins in Marx himself and permeates the twentieth century. This way of delving into Marx, for me, implied a method akin to the "materialism of the encounter," to use Althusser's words. A pure thought of deviation, which reveals the fortuitous combinations that inevitably weave a "sense of the situation," that is, a political thought that allows us to rediscover Marx under the influences of that undercurrent named by Epicurus. In the words of the French philosopher [Louis Althusser], the world appears as "a unique totality that is *not totalised, but experienced in its dispersion*." A strange dispersion, capable of creating something beyond the *system*. And here, Aricó doubles down and suggests thinking in terms of a deviation within the deviation: the construction of the Latin American nation and its relationship with the state from a perspective that does not simply discard Marxism. Of course, for Aricó, the misreading that begins with Marx and that connects with a whole series of subsequent disencounters (crystallised especially with Latin American communist parties) is resolved, or achieves a breaking point, with Gramsci, in a theoretical deviation of Marxism that thinks of the Bolshevik revolution as a revolution against *Capital*. A new deviation from that deviation required a Latin American Gramsci. It was the theories of Peruvian José Carlos Mariátegui that allowed Aricó to say – referring to the socialist movement in Latin America – that in these countries, the *Capital* became "the book of the bourgeoisie," for justifying the necessity and progressiveness of capitalism according to the European model. Aricó puts Marx through the wringer of Gramsci and Mariátegui, and that was the predominant mode of reading Marx in the debate in which I was formed.

Then it was crucial for me to read *Marx más allá de Marx* [in English, *Marx beyond Marx*], by Toni Negri. Here, I found the dispositive of *displacement* to be very productive. Surely *misencounter* and *displacement* share some of the same underlying thread. The readings of Italian *operaismo* on Marx, in particular the re-reading of the *Grundrisse*, have been a key that puts the materialist reflection on the question of "surplus," which leads us to a reading of living labour and its constituent force.

Then, the feminist reading has been fundamental for me: If Marx argues with neoclassical theories to de-fetishise the sphere of circulation, feminists dig deeper and de-fetishise the sphere of production. Thus, they reach the *subsoil* of reproduction. And from there, I was interested in researching the forms and experiences under which social reproduction develops in non-extractive or exploitative terms (which implies a fight against its *naturalisation*). I think I could say that the feminist reading of Marx emphasises, from my point of view, the *differential* of exploitation. With this, we go beyond opposing reproduction and production (as if they were antithetical terms), to think about reorganising their relationship. I had not reflected on it in these terms before, but we can make a triad: *disencounter, displacement, differential*.

We know that several feminists have taken it upon themselves to read Marx in this way. They pursue a double movement and a double objective. On the one hand, to explore hidden places in Marx's work and, on the other hand, and simultaneously, to radicalise Marx's research method of looking into the "hidden abode" of how capitalist reality is produced. The first hidden (and concealed) dimension is reproduction: everything that is both invisible and constitutive of contemporary social production. This is the perspective of Silvia Federici, who describes the "gaps" in Marx that the feminists of the 1970s began to see in his work when they analysed his vision of gender, and then took it upon themselves to reconstruct his categories from their personal political experience of rejecting reproductive work. It is therefore *another origin* of critique. "The feminist movement had to begin with the critique of Marx," Federici always reminds us, and this beginning was driven by political practice. She writes: "I argue that *Wages for Housework* feminists found in Marx the foundation for a feminist theory centred on women's struggle against unpaid domestic labour because we read his analysis of capitalism politically, coming from a direct personal experience, looking for answers to our refusal of domestic relations." More recently, taking Marx's category of the "hidden abode," which is what he calls production in contrast to the "visible" sphere of circulation, Wendy Brown (2006) proposes that feminism must ally itself with critical theory (thinking of the most radical contributions of the Frankfurt School) because that is the way to include these invisible folds in the sphere of production. Here, the "hidden abodes" of production that she highlights are language, psyche, sexuality, aesthetics, reason, and thought itself. Nancy Fraser, in an article titled "Tras la morada oculta de Marx" (2014) [in English, *Behind Marx's Hidden Abode*,] writes that feminism, ecology, and postcolonialism are the three experiential perspectives that reconsider Marxist analysis precisely because they incorporate the "hidden abodes" of social conflict production in contemporary capitalism. In these approaches, the three authors assume – from different positions – a reading of Marx in relation to how the feminist perspective highlights the powers that *produce* the forms of capitalist power as subordination of labour to capital; but even more: how hierarchies function within what we understand as labour. Along this line, they place feminised labour as an example of what capital must subordinate and discredit (that is, *hide*). This symptomatic reading of Marx is a red thread for feminist theory. First, because by taking up the Marxist thread of reproducing the workforce as a necessary activity for capital accumulation, it highlights *the class* dimension of feminism. Then, because it detects in its gaps, abodes, and recesses what Marx left *unthought* precisely because his reading of capital as a social relationship privileges the analysis of production, but not of the production of production (or reproduction). We speak of a *subsoil* of reproduction, from which we see all the layers that ultimately enable what we call the capitalist mode of production. Thus, feminist economics introduces a genuine perspective "from below."

In recent years, there has been a global trend to return to Marxist thought. How can we "return" to Marx considering the specific challenges of current capitalism, as well as the different social struggles and collective bodies?

I think it is a symptom that we have to confront and discuss again, the problem of *liberation* in conditions that need, once again, to be unravelled and elaborated. In other words, practice requires us to do it. As Sandro Mezzadra notes in his book "La cocina de Marx: el sujeto y su producción" [in English, *In the Marxian Workshops: Producing Subjects*] the so-called end of Marxism allowed the Marxist archive to be opened as a polyphony and to re-enter its "workshop." There are core aspects of the Marxian debate that are urgently summoned by our present. One of them is the issue of the so-called "primitive accumulation," with its direct violence and its mode of appropriating common goods. There is a whole body of debate about this, but above all, it seems to me that this has become *thinkable* because there is already a huge and persistent set of anti-extractive struggles that fight against the plundering of land, resources, and the racist and colonial displacement of people, which has created a need for conceptualisation. It is always beautiful to evoke Marx's lines in a letter to S. Mayer at the beginning of 1871, and which are also the spirit of his exchange with Vera Zasulich: "The intellectual movement now taking place in Russia testifies to the fact that fermentation is going on deep below the surface. Minds are always connected by invisible threads with the body of the people." That image of fermentation deep below the surface and invisible threads linked to a popular, subaltern body seems extremely suggestive to me for understanding how the conditions for thought come about. There is a group of Indigenous and Afro intellectuals who have been creating underlying genealogies of reflection for years, which are key for this moment and are also expressed in very powerful political leadership, such as the figures of Berta Cáceres, Marielle Franco, and Francia Márquez, to name a few.

Continuing with the issue of Primitive Accumulation, I am very interested in the financial inflection of capitalism to rethink it in its *current context*. For example, the idea of *unpayable debt*, as framed by Brazilian philosopher Denise Ferreira Da Silva, shows how colonial forces partake in capitalist accumulation through violent expropriations that do not remain confined to the past, a "primitive" or "original" time (thus, she debates Marx's, and even Luxemburg's readings of value). Unpayable debt, Da Silva argues, is a "remembrance" of expropriation. In other words, non-payment becomes possible when the violence of debt is remembered. The dimension of time, as we see, is also central here: It invites the philosopher to introduce the *time* of colonial violence as *actuality* into the Marxian scene of value. She says that this explains the *temporality* that allowed the mortgage debt in 2018 in the United States to be a scam perpetrated against African American families, as their "inability to pay" became a financial asset. Da Silva connects this temporality of debt with two other concerns: the question of the "inheritance" of debt and the possibility of disobedience.

With Luci Cavallero, we wrote *Una lectura feminista de la deuda* [in English, *A Feminist Reading of Debt*]. An analysis of how so-called private debt and/or household debt is in fact a form of exploitation of the most precarious, usually feminised and migrant labour. In the light of the feminist mobilisation of recent years, we researched how women, lesbians, transvestites, and transsexuals do not fit in as a universal subject of debt, but how the precariousness of their jobs, the burden of obligatory unpaid work, and the macho violence that is often linked to the lack of economic autonomy are exploited in a *differential* way. A *differential* of "financial exploitation" is added to the sexual and racial division of labour, translating into sources of debt, interest rates, and different allocations of debt. This also allowed us to concretise the notion of domestic debt in relation to specific configurations of households, which are no longer predominantly organised under a heteropatriarchal family structure. In the domestic sphere, a "sexual division of debt" is *already* at work, which is obscured when households are only addressed in general terms. With this, I want to emphasise the collective struggles led by concrete subjects against forms of dispossession and exploitation that exceed, reconfigure, and update conflict dynamics.

The revolutionary subject is a central component within Marxism and the Left more broadly. However, as you mention in several of your texts, we cannot re-

duce this subject to an androcentric perspective centred on the factory. How can we think about revolutionary subjects today?

The current situation forces us to discuss the renewed forms of capitalist violence. One concrete way of charting them is to trace where the "civil war" between labour and capital is waged today. According to Marx, it occurred during the workday, but today, this battlefield is actually widening and expanding, in both territorial (beyond the factory) and temporal terms (beyond the usual work hours). What forms of violence does this civil war take today if we look at it from a social cooperation perspective that sees informalised, migrant, and popular economies, and domestic-community work as keys to new proletarian areas in neoliberalism? We do not have to abandon our reading of neoliberalism as the so-called workers' conflict (instead of a farewell to the proletariat), but we must do so outside its usual coordinates (a wage-earning, unionised, masculine framework), and think of the expansion of the financial system as a simultaneous response to a specific sequence of struggles and, on the other hand, a dynamic of containment that structures a certain experience of the current crisis.

In my book *la potencia feminista* [in English, *Feminist International*,] I addressed this by trying to connect four scenes of violence: 1) The implosion of violence in homes as an effect of the crisis of the figure of the male breadwinner, and his subsequent loss of authority and privileged role in relation to his position in the labour market; 2) the organisation of new forms of violence as a principle of authority in popular-sector neighbourhoods, rooted in the expansion of illegal economies that replace other modes of provisioning resources; 3) the dispossession and looting of common lands and resources by transnational corporations, and thus the deprivation of the material autonomy of other economies; and 4) the articulation of forms of exploitation and value extraction for which the financialisation of social life – particularly through the apparatus of debt – is a common code. I consider that from each concrete struggle against the forms of violence expressed in these situations, there are subjects who lead and sustain them. It is, therefore, about reading existing conflicts and from there, the subjects in struggle that inhabit and sustain them, rather than *first* thinking about the existence of a revolutionary subject that we should *then* seek. It is also a way of *not immobilising ourselves or waiting* for the emergence of some abstract notion of ideal subjects. This, of course, does not resolve the problem of political subjectivities.

We are seeing that the current ultra-Right mobilises anti-elitist feelings and meanings from which they seek to galvanise, especially those who have the experience of daily war, and especially among those who are also stripped of their role as providers and bearers of hierarchies guaranteed by a patriarchal system. This has been an important element in recent feminist debates to explain domestic violence and what we call the implosion of households.

If the hypothesis that we have been working on with Silvia Federici – which is formulated in our joint book *¿Quién le debe a quién?* – is that we are facing *a restructuring of class relations whose main scene is the sphere of reproduction*, then we have to read the neoliberal mutations there. This gives rise to a major problem that I consider an open question for feminisms: What are the political tools of protest and negotiation of a workforce that is at the crossroads between financial (and platforms) capitalism and unguaranteed social reproduction?

In the current context, it seems increasingly difficult to talk about internationalism given that many emancipatory political projects are confined to the local or national level, or articulate their demands around identities. Where do you see potentials of forging these struggles into a transnational movement?

I believe these are already transnational struggles, and yet, we still have to consider what it means to sustain them, translate them, articulate them. The cycle of feminist mobilisations and organisation that began internationally in 2016 has managed to consolidate a growing cycle of social mobilisations in the years 2017, 2018, and 2019. The strikes in Poland and Argentina that took place in 2016 are intertwined with mobilisations that had just begun, such as *Ni Una Menos* in Argentina in 2015, and have been gaining even more momentum. I even argue that strikes are a tool to change their political quality, surpassing an organisational threshold. By 2017, March 8 had become an international feminist strike with various forms of organisation in dozens of countries, including mobilisations that are true milestones in certain countries such as Chile, Mexico, Spain, and Italy, to name a few. In this three-year period from 2017 to 2019, a movement has been *scaling up* because: 1) the feminist strike of March 8 is organised and consolidated; 2) the internationalist character of the movement is expanding, with a clear impulse from the South; 3) it is linked to international campaigns for the right to abortion; 4) the feminist movement converges with popular and Indigenous protest dynamics in several Latin American countries.

I would like to insist on a point I also argue in my book: the transnational dynamics in which feminist struggles are rooted already exist. On the one hand, there are *domestic territories*, which are today spaces of practical transnationalism, where global chains of care are assembled, where we discuss modes of invisibilisation of reproductive work and the lack of public infrastructure that causes them to bear the cost of adjustment. Then, *Indigenous and community territories*, historically expropriated and considered to be closed, "backward" economies, are today spaces of borderless alliances, of community support, where extractive megaprojects and the new landowners in charge of agribusiness are denounced. From these territories, we can trace the global diagram of the extractive dynamics of capital, opposed by alliances, struggles, and networks to resist and expel these neocolonial advances. Finally, *territories of precarisation*. Historically considered "unorganised," they are today forms of experimentation of new trade union dynamics, of encampments and occupations in workshops and factories and on virtual platforms, of creative demands and denunciations that make explicit how sexual abuse, discrimination against migrants, and exploitation always go hand in hand.

We must acknowledge that they bear the brunt of the most aggressive dynamic of the conservative, patriarchal, and racist counter-offensive.

If we understand neo-fascism in relation to what it responds to, to how it fabricates enemies in order to legitimise its intervention and its proposal for subjectivation, we must underscore its capacity to deploy and mobilise what, together with Gabriel Giorgi, we call forms of *reactive transgression*. Thus, on the one hand, we see an ability to mobilise the cultural prestige and the seductive capacity of transgression, undoubtedly inherited from the twentieth century, to use it in specific directions, corresponding to the values and modelling of the public that these new Right-wing forces seek to consolidate and spread: hyperindividualism, so-called "antipolitics," the free market and its relentless grammars of racism, masculinism, and classism. Yet, on the other hand, we argue that it is a transgression that seeks to replicate and compete in the realm of the disruptive with the challenges that transfeminisms pose, not only in cultural terms, but also at the political, economic, and subjective levels. We could add that this politics, which likes to present itself as anti-establishment in its reaction, claims to offer a "realistic" balance of how recent democratic dynamics have combined with forms of inclusion, while the majorities require a subjectivation that is trained in the arenas of neoliberal competitiveness. Here, as we see, we are dealing with struggles that are simultaneously local and transnational.

In your book "Feminist International" (2020), you give great centrality to the strike, especially the feminist strike as a process, as a cartography of feminist practice. What new readings do you give to the strikes that have taken place in Argentina (for example, the one on January 24, 2024) in rejection of Javier Milei's ultra-Right government policies? What bodies, emotions, and demands are being articulated?

Through the strike, the feminist movement decisively politicises the crisis of reproduction in the neoliberal moment, making visible both the scale of unpaid feminised work and its convergence with processes of precarisation. It also makes explicit and confronts the gender orders that structure this precariousness. I, of course, was interested in how the notion of strike is displaced and reinvented, expanding the notion of labour, broadening the very notion of class from below. The strike has become a strategy to make visible and value the labour trajectories that remain unrecognised. The feminist strike is a collective exercise that questions the patriarchal concept of wage-labour. Moreover, such valorisation of social reproduction implies the recognition of other spatialities that are not confined to the household.

Milei's election was quickly followed by an attack on living conditions by way of a decree announced on December 20, the date of the popular revolt of 2001. Since then, there have been *cacerolazos* and protests. On January 24, just a month and a half after he took office, trade unions called for a general strike. To participate in that strike, we organised a huge feminist assembly, which was an important instance to discuss a diagnosis and a plan of action. It was also an anticipation of the assembly process towards March 8 that we initiated in February.

What happened on March 8 was impressive for several reasons. First, because we managed to recover a pre-pandemic level of attendance. Then, because we did it against an ultra-Right government, which constantly denigrates women in general and feminisms in particular. Thirdly, because we organised ourselves in the face of a severe and brand-new repressive protocol, against which we "flooded" the streets and decentralised in a fully coordinated way. Self-care worked perfectly among us and was part of the reflection and tasks undertaken during the whole assembly process. Finally, as I have already pointed out, because we are in the midst of an economic war against the population, which makes organising and mobilising a huge challenge. This is why the massive scale of 8M 2024 in Argentina is extremely valuable and powerful.

I would like to return to your experience as a feminist militant in *Ni Una Menos* and to the recent events of March 8. What challenges are being articulated within the movement in the current context in Argentina? How is the *Feminist Potencia* being remade?

I wrote a weekly chronicle of what was discussed in the assemblies, of the challenges that emerged, of the difficulties and proposals that were being woven.

In each of them, it was clear that the brutal advance against wages, rights, and possibilities of communal life do not go uncontested from below, from consolidated organisational forms of protest to jumping turnstiles in the subway in response to a hike in transit fares. Milei using electric appliances as metaphors for the virulence of his "anarcho-capitalist" government – the blender and the chainsaw – translates the shock of the country's accelerated impoverishment, including the lowest wage level in Argentine history. The assembly is also a forum for collective writing, where different concepts appear, others are reengaged, and we "cook" a new language for protest in a moment that is unprecedented and in which words often seem insufficient or escape us in the dizzying craze of everyday life.

I want to explore how the feminist assembly, as a political body, has a mode that is both continuous and discontinuous. We are now in the space that, despite all the difficulties of articulating heterogeneity, has been sustained since 2016. It functions as a coordinating instance of a movement that stands out for combining political structures, collectives of various types, and "independent" participants. The uniting factor is that shared platform to discuss the current situation and organise the streets. The assembly may have reiterative modes and performances, but it gives a different response each time; it deploys contextual intelligence to mix and enhance voices and experiences that would not otherwise meet in political conversation if it were purely virtual or segmented by pre-organised sectors.

The priority this year was to highlight the issue of hunger and to showcase the women who are sustaining the *ollas populares* (in English, collective kitchens or soup kitchens) that feed 10 million people today. The assembly expresses what the feminist movement has achieved in these years like no other: to speak simultaneously of waged and unwaged work, registered and unregistered, visible and invisible, domestic and communal. It is, in fact, what has allowed the feminist strikes of March 8 to include many of those realities that must strive to *invent* a way to strike and be recognised in this *absence* of tasks that are generally not considered work.

What is to be done? We are entering a stage in which popular feminisms in Argentina assume the challenge of changing the fabric of communal life, which the crisis has been attacking for a long time now, which has been infiltrated by this idea of sacrifice at the expense of leisure, where joy and pleasure are censured while cruelty is celebrated, where violence is imposed against solidarity and mutual support.

Finally, how have you overcome what has become an entrenched divide between theory and political practice? How have you built militant research?

I do not think it is something that can be "overcome" because there is a fixed system in which you have to divide your time and specialise, or dedicate yourself to either one thing or another. And, as we know, the more precarious our lives become, the more we are forced to "manage" our time. That is why I am interested in the experience of militant research as a practice that challenges boundaries; that does not confine thought exclusively to academic spaces, nor assumes that politics does not require thought because it is *already* known, and that increasingly requires a delicate production of availability, time, and commitment.

For me, it is a practice, as well, from where to combat anti-intellectual prejudice, which has a great impact on intellectuals and militants and has managed to sediment a series of commonplaces that are still operating. For example, the outdated division between thinking and doing; between elaborating and experimenting; between comfort and risk. These are undoubtedly poles that produce caricatures: the militant self-denial for practice, as if it were devoid of ideas, and the intellectuals' pristine adoration of the realm of concepts, as if it were a pure abstraction.

Despite the stereotypical nature of these figures, they continue to mark the boundaries of a map that, however, has changed a lot.

I am very interested in how in this cycle of massive and radical mobilisations of feminisms, that division into intellectual, conceptional, and political is changing. The question about anti-intellectual prejudice can also be posed the other way around: Every time this binary (in its most brutal formula: those who do and those who think) re-emerges, we see a disciplinary response to any shift in the relationship between thought and practice. Therefore, anti-intellectualism, instead of being a nod to the popular and its experiential richness (as it is often portrayed), is a call to order and a confirmation of classist, sexist, and racist hierarchies.

In a recent text published in a feminist compilation, I argued about the feminist movement's "desire for theory". It's something that interests me a lot. When I refer to the feminist movement's desire for theory, I mean our capacity to return to a magnificent era due to a collective capacity to raise problems, broach them, and address them in a way that does not involve linear solutions. But it does produce the experience of formulating them, of being part of their redefinition, all the way to the edges of the thinkable, and without resorting to the shortcuts of other formulas that seem more expeditious. Thus, a capacity for "reflective indocility" is redeployed, to use the Foucauldian term, as a diffuse sensitivity that makes conceptualisation a practice linked to disobedience.

Then, that desire for theory relates to the dynamic of creating names and narratives for what needs to be said differently. Undoubtedly, this versatility with this conceptual language expresses a capacity to make practice an interrogative form, with marches and countermarches, trial and errors. It is not by chance, as bell hooks said, that "feminist willingness to change direction when needed has been a major source of strength and vitality in feminist struggle," also in other historical moments. The intimacy with that ability to venture into speaking in a new language, criticising oneself, reopening past debates, is related to the vitality of a movement that thinks while it moves. Thus, thought is an attribute of movement. bell hooks adds that "our theory must remain fluid, open, responsive to new information" to be in tune with changes in our lives. That fluidity filled with theoretical substance enriches the movement. But also, I want to add that this cycle we are talking about, that conceptualisation is driven strongly from the South.

I believe that in that desire for theory, there is strategy and concern for mass-scale pedagogy. In this context, we also recognise the reactionary alarm, which makes language, content, and educational forms preferred targets for attacks and counteroffensives by the far Right when it seeks to combat so-called "gender ideology."

Part II
Embodied Subjects

Another Pregnancy is Possible: Making Surrogacy Unthinkable (by Universalising Surrogacy)[1]

Sophie Lewis

This is a plea for speculative attention to what I propose we frame as the *problem of human pregnancy*. There is a real need for new discourses, artworks and fabulations that make visible how weird it is that, as a society, we do not generally organize research into ways to potentially alleviate the obvious problem, which is that – as Shulamith Firestone put it succinctly in 1970 – pregnancy "isn't good for you" (Firestone 1970: 198). Notwithstanding the pleasure that many people take in the experience, gestating a human fetus is a form of labour that claims the lives of an estimated 300,000 adults every year, which is about a seventh of the number of people the International Labour Organization estimates succumb annually to "work-related accidents or diseases."[2] Why, then, is it unremarkable for a person with a potentially implantable uterus to walk around *sans* contraceptive pill, *sans* IUD? Why is it acceptable for societies *not* to invest every possible resource into minimizing the dangers pregnancy poses to those who are pregnant? Why is experimental development of ectogenetic (artificial womb) devices such as the "BioBag," proven so far on fetal sheep, justified only in terms of saving "preemies"? The fact that it is thinkable to ask (or expect) a person to do pregnancy at all, let alone for significantly less than $1 an hour, ought to stun us.

The new global trend towards commercial "surrogacy" does less than nothing to address the problem of pregnancy. If anything, with its tendency to subject waged gestators to risky multiple-embryo transfers, it intensifies it. Ges-

---

1   This article was first published in: Lewis, Sophie (2023) "Another Pregnancy is Possible: Making Surrogacy Unthinkable (by Universalizing Surrogacy)." In: Marina Vishmidt (ed.), Speculation, Boston: MIT, pp.98-107. Reproduced with permission of the author.
2   International Labour Organization, World Statistic: "The enormous burden of poor working conditions", 15 November, 2015.

tational surrogates are pregnancy contractors who work in an industrial sector often misleadingly referred to as "Assisted Reproduction" (as though reproduction were ever unassisted!): they are discursively positioned as the technology component of the service we call "assisted reproductive technology." They are enlisted as pure *techne* – uncreative muscle – for it is the genetic commissioners who are paying for the privilege of "authorship." In general, even while *on* the job, surrogacy workers don't receive meaningful healthcare benefits, i.e., ones that aren't simply about safeguarding the fetus – albeit the distinction is blurry, given that a fetus is a part of a gestator's body. What is crystal clear is that capitalist "infertility solutions" have little to do with refusals by some fractions of the population in the Global North to do gestational labour. Rather, they represent a response to a market demand for genetic parenthood. Pregnancy work is not so much disappearing or getting easier as being outsourced: crashing through various regulatory barriers onto an open market. As ever, capitalism is not solving the problem, only moving it around. Let the poor do the dirty work, wherever they are cheapest (or most convenient) to enrol.

And no wonder, given that the ground for such a development was already being laid as early as the late nineteenth century, when large swathes of the colonial, upper-class, frequently women-led eugenics movement in Europe and North America argued that the best way to realize pregnancy's promise – namely, a thriving future "race" achieved through sexual "virtue" and white-supremacist "hygiene" – was for the state to economically discipline all sexual activity unconducive to that horizon.[3] As good social democrats, these "feminist" progressives wanted a nation-state that was duty-bound to feed, shelter, clothe, educate, and train the gestational labourers present within its territory, and (especially) the products of that gestational labor. Since this was then, and remains now, a costly sounding proposition, a set of enduring ideas and policies were propagated around the turn of the century, according to which, as far as metropolitan proletarians were concerned, having babies spells financial irresponsibility and surefire ruin in and of itself – especially out of wedlock. The same discouragement applied, more or less, to nonwhite (Italian, Irish, Arab) immigrants on the eastern American seaboard, with Black, Latinx, disabled and otherwise "unfit" populations suffering the brunt of sterilization drives – a practice which continues to this day in US Immigration and Customs Enforcement (Ice) detention centers (The Guardian 2020). Lumpenproletarian populations in "the colonies" (notably India) were first

---

3   On eugenic feminism, see: Schuller 2021; Newman 1999; Nadkarni 2014.

incentivized to "control" their reproduction, and then targeted later for their outsource-able fertility. Curiously, for families of the capitalist class, having babies has always signified a virtuous and vital investment guaranteeing their – and the very economy's – good fortunes.

"That there is even a relationship between material well-being and child-bearing is a twentieth-century, middle-class, and to some extent white belief," historian Laura Briggs insists (2017: 127). Nevertheless, it's been but a series of logical steps from that hegemonic notion of reproductive meritocracy to the beginnings of the pregnancy "gig" economy we can glimpse today. In unprecedentedly literal ways, people make babies for others in exchange for the money required to underwrite morally, as well as materially, their own otherwise barely justifiable baby-having. It's not quite accurate, though, to say that the basic ideas of early eugenicist reproductive policy have *resurfaced* in late capitalism – or even to say that they've survived. Rather, as W. E. B. Du Bois lays out in *Black Reconstruction in America*, these interlocking logics of property and sub-humanity, privatization, and punishment, form the template that organized capitalism in the first place and sustains it as a system (Du Bois 1999). Dominant liberal-democratic discourses that hype a world of post-racial values and bootstrap universality only serve to render dispossessed populations the more responsible for their trespass of being alive and having kids while black. Stratification is self-reproducing and not designed to be resolved.

It is still educational to call out contemporary iterations of eugenic common sense for their face-value incoherence; still legitimate to point out (the hypocrisy!) that even as urban working-class and black motherhood continues to come under attack, the barriers to Black and working-class women's access to contraception and abortion grow steadily more formidable. The positive "choice" to "freely invest" in having a baby is one that numerous laws are literally forcing many people to make, with dire and frequently fatal results. Obstetric care in India remains to this day among the scantest in the whole world – even though India exports and offers obstetric medical care to customers around the world. Such contradictions, as Melinda Cooper details in her account of the speculative logics of the "biotech" economy, *Life As Surplus*, are part and parcel of capitalist geopolitical economy – which needs populations to extinguish in the process of making others thrive (Cooper 2008). The account of the booming bioeconomy of "living material" detailed by Cooper offers a prism that enables us to see the predatory logic of financialized capitalism as a question, not only of uneven value driving the global division of racialized living labour, nor simply "human capital" in neoliberal terms, but of access to *life* as a side-effect of accumulation. It's not just life that is a sexually transmitted disease, as the old joke has it. Birth justice campaigners know, as indeed AIDS activists knew in the 1980s and 1990s, that it is death that sex spreads, simultaneously, in the context of for-profit health care.

However, this depressing state of affairs hasn't ever been the whole story. The "speculation" of which gestational labor is capable has multiple, perhaps even communizing, valences. From Soviet mass holiday camps for pregnant comrades, to Germany's inventive (albeit doomed) "twilight sleep" methods – designed to completely erase the memory of labour pain – not to mention over a hundred years of scientific prediction and science-fiction about ectogenesis and its imminent revolutionary social consequences, human history contains a plethora of ambitious ideologies and technological experiments for liberating and collectivising childbirth. It's admittedly an ambivalent record. Irene Lusztig, director of a beautiful 2013 archival film on this subject, has understandably critical words for the various early-twentieth-century rest-camps and schools of childbirth she discusses (Lusztig 2013). But, she suggests, you have to hand it to them – even the most wrongheaded of textbooks written a century ago at least stated the problem to be solved in uncompromising terms: "Birth injuries are so common that Nature must intend for women to be used up in the process of reproduction, just as a salmon die after spawning." (ibid)

Well if that's what Nature intends, the early utopian midwives and medical reformers featured in *The Motherhood Archives* responded: then Nature is an ass. Why accept Nature as natural? If this is what childbirth is "naturally" like, they reasoned, looking about them in the maternity wards of Europe and America, then it quite obviously needs to be denatured, remade. Easier said than done. Pioneering norms of fertility care based on something like cyborg self-determination have turned out to be a moving target. The exceptionality and careworthiness of gestation remains something that has to be forcibly naturalized, spliced in against the grain of a "Nature" whose fundamental indifference to death, injury, and suffering does not, paradoxically, come naturally to most of us.

Many of these efforts to emancipate humanity from gestational "Nature" claimed the name of "Nature" for their cause, too. For instance, the turn to so-called "natural childbirth" – which earned such fiery contempt from Firestone, the founder of New York Radical Women, for being bourgeois – more accurately stands for a regimen full of carefully stylized gestational labor hacks and artifices, a suite of mental and physical conditioning that may be billed as "intuitive" but which nevertheless take time and skill to master. "Natural childbirth" has never gone entirely out of fashion and is still extremely popular among diverse social classes. Particular subdoctrines of natural childbirth continue to come under well-justified fire wherever they stray into mystification – some ecofeminists, for instance, are rightly criticized by xenofeminists for romanticizing loss of bodily autonomy (Hester 2019: 37–40)[4]. However, the broader free-birthing movement's foundational critique of just-in-time capitalist obstetrics and its colonial-patriarchal history (whereby midwives, witches, and their indigenous knowledges were expelled from the gestational workplace) is hard to fault.[5]

I have no quarrel with the world's trans-inclusive autonomist midwives and radical doulas, the ones lobbying for their work to become a guaranteed form of free health care rather than a profitable profession. I have no quarrel with "full-spectrum" birth-work that supports people of all genders through abortion, miscarriage, fertility treatments, labor, and postpartum, often operating outside of biomedical establishments, spreading bottom-up mutual aid, disseminating methods geared toward achieving minimally (that is, sufficiently) medicated, maximally pleasurable reproduction. Power to them. With their carefully refined systems of education, training, and traditional lay science, they are, in their own way, creating a nature worth fighting for. It can hardly be an accident that, as anyone who spends time in midwifery networks will realize, so many of them are anti-authoritarian communists.

But let's not forget to demand the impossible with regard to birth. Critical utopianisms require us to struggle in, against, and beyond the present state of things. Where are we now? Few people consciously want babies to be commodities. Yet baby commodities are a definite part of what gestational labor produces today. Given the variety of organizing principles that can apply to the baby assembly line, it is ahistorical (at best) to claim that what we produce when we're pregnant is simply "life," love, or "synthetic value": the value of human knitted-togetherness (O'Brien 1981). Such claims are unsatisfying, in the first instance, because they fail to account for gestators who do not bond with what's inside them. And they can't fully grasp altruistic surrogacy, where the goal is explicitly to not generate a bond between gestator and baby in the course of the labor (even if some surrogates do attach and sometimes propose a

---

4   Helen Hester critically unpacks Maria Mies's view of pregnancy.
5   For examples of literature written from the "free-birthing" or "natural childbirth" wing of the reproductive justice movement, refer to: Mahoney, Mary/Mitchell, Lauren (2016).

less exclusive, open adoption–style parenting model after they've given birth). The related, philosophically widespread, claim that social bonds are grounded biologically in pregnancy – what some call the "nine-month head-start" to a relationship – is ultimately incomplete. The better question is surely: a head-start to what? What type of social bonds are grounded by which approach to pregnancy?

Clearly, if I am gestating a fetus, I may feel that I am in relationship with that (fetal) part of my body. That "relationship" may even ground the sociality that emerges around me and the infant if and when it is born, assuming that we continue to cohabit. But I may also conceptualize the work in a completely different way – grounding an alternate social world. I may never so much as see (or wish to see) my living product; am I not still grounding a bond with the world through that birth? For that matter, people around me may fantasize that they are in a relationship with the interior of my bump, and they will even be "right" insofar as the leaky contamination and synchronization of bodies, hormonally and epigenetically, takes place in many (as yet insufficiently understood) ways. We simply cannot generalize about "the social" without knowing the specifics of the labor itself. And, regardless of the "ground" the gestational relationship provides, the fabric of the social is something we ultimately weave by taking up where gestation left off, encountering one another as the strangers we always are, adopting one another skin-to-skin, forming loving and abusive attachments, and striving at comradeship. To say otherwise is to naturalize and thus, ironically, to devalue that ideological shibboleth "the mother-fetus bond." What if we reimagined pregnancy, and not just its prescribed aftermath, as work under capitalism – that is, as something to be struggled in, against, and beyond, toward a utopian horizon free of work and free of value?

Crucial to any antiwork "Aufhebung" of pregnancy will be our collective abolition of private property as it exists within kinship. That human beings are the products of gestational labour does not mean that a "nonalienated" relation between the labourer and her "fruits" is a property relation: *you are my child*. (The promissory reward of capitalist pregnancy is, in Firestone's terms, a "baby all your own to fuck up as you please.") Let us remember, instead, the insights of the Third World Lesbian and Gay caucuses, the interracial Black lesbian mothers writing in *Off Our Backs!* in the Seventies, Sisterhood of Black Single Mothers, and the family-abolitionist wings of gay and women's liberation: that children *do not belong to anyone* except insofar as they belong to everyone, which is to say, they "belong only to themselves" (Peña/Carey 1979:

9). Let us assume that is possible for any of us to learn that it is the holders – not the delusional "authors," self-replicators, and "patenters" – who truly people the world.

Holding bodies as fluid as human beings' bodies is difficult, slippery labour. I have offered "amniotechnics" as a term for the watery art of holding and caring even while being ripped into, at the same time as being held (Lewis 2017)[6]. Amniotechnics is protecting water and protecting people from water, protecting the water that *is* people, as well as the water that is not (currently) people, *from* people. Our wateriness, I suggest in my first family-abolition manifesto, is our "surrogacy."[7] It is the bed of our bodies' overlap and it is, not necessarily – but possibly – a source of comradeliness. To an extent, bodies are always leaky, parasited, and nonunitary, as the vital and varied flora of bacteria in every body, not just gestating ones, demonstrates. In the accounts of earthly life given by biologists such as Lynn Margulis, we are all revealed to be disconcertingly pregnant with myriad entities, bacteria, viruses, and more, some of whom are even simultaneously gestating us. It's not safe nor is it pretty: to accept the world as fluid is also to accept fluidity's price.

"Water management" may sound unexciting, but I suspect it contains key secrets to the kinmaking practices of the future. Just as with water, we've consented too much to the privatization of procreativity. Just as with water, we've taken kinship for granted, imagining it as something that is given, not made. Reproductive justice and water justice are inseparable. The substance of this connection, however, is often wrongly ascribed to the type of primitivism-tinged ecofeminism that too often roots its claims in tacitly colonial and sex-essentialist imaginaries of nature so as to be non-challenging to settler environmentalists and white allies. By way of antidote, we might consider the framing of water offered by the radical midwife Wicanhpi Iyotan Win Autumn

---

6   Adapted as Chapter 7 of *Full Surrogacy Now: Feminism Against Family* (Lewis 2019). The essay "Amniotechnics" has also been re-printed in a volume of essays and poetry, put together via the study group Matter in Flux and the research collective The World In Which We Occur. See: Teets, Jennifer (ed.) (2021). "Amniotechnics" also constitutes the basis of an iris-printed broadsheet by Johanna Ehde and Elisabeth Rafstedt, who spliced the text together with "Triple Jeopardy," an early 1970s newspaper by Frances Beal and others in the Third World Women's Alliance. See: Rietlanden Women's Office (2020) *MsHeresies #3*. "Amniotechnics" appears, finally, in Denisa Tomková (ed.) (2022) *Kunsthalle Bratislava Online Publication*.

7   A second, shorter, manifesto, *Abolish the Family: A Manifesto for Care and Liberation*, was published by Verso Books in 2022.

Lavender-Wilson, who theorizes "amniotechnics" with the help of a long line of decolonial science and materialism:

> It was through the work of Fanon and Memmi, LaDuke and Deloria, that I came to midwifery. As Dakota people, we understand that *mni wiconi* is not some fluffy abstract concept designed to fuel some hokey pseudo-spiritual practice. [C]lean water has the power to heal, contaminated water has the power to kill.[8]

For me, these words illuminate amniotic water as something that "complexity" theorist John Urry might call a "global fluid" (Urry 2002). Rather than equate water with a universal concept of 'life,' Wicanhpi approaches liquid as the historical ground of life in particular. Techniques for curating amniotic water, as she suggests, must integrate the dual meaning of 'care' (pain and relief) and the double power of medicine (poison and cure).

> We have to make sure there isn't too much, or too little [amniotic water]. From the lead-contaminated water poisoning the children of Flint, Michigan, to cancer caused by [perfluorooctanoic acid] contamination in the water of Hoosick Falls, New York, to Newark public schools giving lead-contaminated water to their entire student and staff population ... to the consequences of uranium mining, nuclear waste facilities, fracking, oil spills and outdated public works systems ... [water politics] is and has been a lived reality for many Indigenous nations for the past several decades.[9]

Crucial to the practical awareness of pregnancy's liquid molecular joy and violence is, as Dakota midwives like Wicanhpi suggest, a consciousness of its embeddedness in global structures of social reproduction. Pregnancy is bound up with colonialism, white supremacy, capital, and gender – but also resistance.

A communist amniotechnics would unbuild the fantasy of an aseptic separation between all these spaces and entities. It would be the art of timing desired or needful openings between them that are savvy, safer, and conducive

---

8   Changing Woman Intitative Blog (2016) "Mni Wiconi Yaktan k'a Ni Drink the Water of Life, and Live," by Wicanhpi Iyotan Win Autumn Lavender-Wilson, 6 August (https://web.archive.org/web/20170604072700/http://www.changingwomaninitiative.com/blog/-mni-wiconi-yaktan-ka-ni-drink-the-water-of-life-and-live).

9   Ibid.

to flourishing. Surrogates to the front! By surrogates, I mean all those comradely gestators, midwives, and other sundry interveners in the more slippery moments of social reproduction: repairing boats; swimming across borders; blockading lake-threatening pipelines; carrying; miscarrying. Let's all learn right now how comradely beings can help plan, mitigate, interrupt, suffer, and reorganize this amniotic violence. Let's think how we can assist in this regenerative wet-wrestling, sharing out its burden.

Recognizing our inextricably surrogated contamination with and by everybody else (and everybody else's babies) will not so much "smash" the nuclear family as make it unthinkable. And that's what needs to happen if we are serious about reproductive justice, which is to say, serious about revolution. There's a world worth living in, unfurling liquidly through the love and rage of – among other things – contract gestators' refusal to be temporary. For surrogates to enter the realm of the political is necessarily to abolish the concept of surrogation (*standing in, in place of the proper body*). For surrogates to struggle is to begin to render the concept of "surrogacy" unthinkable (as it should be) and the property relation untenable. It is to challenge to the logic of hierarchical "assistance," and a premonition of genuine mutuality. Speculatively, hopefully, we might call it an invading mode of life based on mutual aid.

For if babies were universally thought of as anybody and everybody's responsibility, "belonging" to nobody, surrogacy would not only generate no profits – it would cease to make sense at the most basic level. Wouldn't the question then simply be: how can baby making best be distributed and made to realize collective needs and desires?

Formal gestational workers' self-interest, like that of their unpaid counterparts, is an anti-work matter, and anti-work in the domain of care production is admittedly sometimes bloody. Their tacit threat to reproductive capitalism, whose knowledges and machinery they embody, takes the world a few steps toward anti-propertarian polymaternalism. Terrifyingly and thrillingly, it whispers the promise of the reproductive commune. Two decades ago, more or less, my father told my brother and me that, no, actually, he would not love us if we were revealed to be, genetically speaking, "the children of the milkman" rather than "his kids." I can still feel the abyssal alienation of that moment. Yet, equally, in the aspirationally universal queer love of my friendship networks, in my queerly held and polymaternally tended flesh, I can sense the mutations of an incipient communization. Everywhere about me, I can see beautiful militants hell-bent on regeneration, not self-replication.

References

Briggs, Laura (2017): How All Politics Became Reproductive Politics, Berkeley, CA: University of California Press.

Bryant, Miranda (2020): "Allegations of Unwanted Ice Hysterectomies Recall Grim Time in US History." In: The Guardian, September 21, 2020 (http://theguardian.com/us-news/2020/sep/21/unwanted-hysterectomy-allegations-ice-georgia-immigration).

Changing Woman Intitative Blog (2016): "Mni Wiconi Yaktan k'a Ni Drink the Water of Life, and Live," by Wicanhpi Iyotan Win Autumn Lavender-Wilson, 6 August 2016. (https://web.archive.org/web/20170604072700/http://www.changingwomaninitiative.com/blog/-mni-wiconi-yaktan-ka-ni-drink-the-water-of-life-and-live)

Cooper, Melinda (2008): Life as Surplus: Biotechnology and Capitalism in the Neoliberal Era, Seattle: University of Washington Press.

Du Bois, W.E.B. (1999 [1935]): Black Reconstruction in America 1860–1880, New York: Free Press.

Firestone, Shulamith (1970): The Dialectic of Sex: The Case for Feminist Revolution, New York: William Morrow.

Gumbs, Alexis Pauline (2016): "M/Other Ourselves: A Black Queer Feminist Genealogy for Radical Mothering." In: Alexis Pauline Gumbs/China Williams/Mai'a Martens (eds.), Revolutionary Mothering: Love on the Front Lines, Oakland, CA: PM Press, pp. 21–31.

Hester, Helen (2019): Xenofeminism, Cambridge and Medford MA: Polity Press.

Lewis, Sophie (2017): "Amniotechnics." In: The New Inquiry, January 25, 2017 (http://thenewinquiry.com/amniotechnics/).

Lewis, Sophie (2019): Full Surrogacy Now: Feminism Against Family, London/New York: Verso.

Lusztig, Irene (dir.) (2013): The Motherhood Archives, US, 91min, (http://wmm.com/catalog/film/the-motherhood-archives).

Mahoney, Mary/Mitchell, Lauren (2016): The Doulas: Radical Care for Pregnant People, CUNY, New York: The Feminist Press.

Nadkarni, Asha (2014): Eugenic Feminism: Reproductive Nationalism in the United States and India, Minneapolis: University of Minnesota Press.

Newman, Louise (1999): White Women's Rights: The Racial Origins of Feminism in the United States, New York: Oxford University Press.

O'Brien, Mary (1981): The Politics of Reproduction, London: Unwin Hyman.

Peña, Mary/Carey, Barbara (1979): "Lesbian Sisters on Racism." off our backs #9.

Rietlanden Women's Office (2020): *MsHeresies* #3 (https://rietlanden.womensoffice.nl/).

Schuller, Kyla (2021): The Trouble with White Women, New York: Bold Type Books.

Teets, Jennifer (ed.) (2021): Electric Brine, Berlin: Archive Books.

The Guardian (2020): "Allegations of Unwanted Ice Hysterectomies Recall Grim Time in US history", September 21, 2020 (http://theguardian.com/us-news/2020/sep/21/unwanted-hysterectomy-allegations-ice-georgia-immigration).

Tomková, Denisa (ed). (2023): Wandering Concepts / Putujúce koncepty. Bratislava: Kunsthalle Bratislava.

Urry, John (2002): Global Complexity, London: Polity Press.

Alienation in Christian Schmacht's *Fleisch mit weißer Soße* (2017)

Ivo Zender

1. Introduction

In this chapter, I revisit Marx's concept of alienation within the context of contemporary trans literature, specifically focusing on Christian Schmacht's *Fleisch mit weißer Soße* (2017). Schmacht portrays the experiences of his protagonist and narrator Chrissy, who earns his living as a sex worker, while also grappling with his trans identity. Through this literary work, I explore how alienation intersects with the unique struggles of trans sex workers in a capitalist society.

Fleisch mit weißer Soße conveys Chrissy's experiences over the course of one year in the form of a fragmentary diary. Chrissy is a white trans man, working in a Berlin brothel under his female persona, Leonie. The difficulties of living in a capitalist, cisheteropatriarchal, racist, ableist and femme-phobic society, leave him feeling deeply isolated, depressed and alienated from everything and everyone. His improving mental state towards the narrative's end, however, raises questions about the potential for regaining agency.

Rooted in the affective, literature serves as an ideal tool for deepening our understanding of alienation. Through the act of reading, it allows us to emotionally explore how capitalism intersects with oppressive structures such as race, gender, sexuality or disability. As a form of art, literature sensually captures the embodied experiences of individuals, revealing the affective currents that impact workers' bodies and reflecting the realities of contemporary capitalism through language and narrative.

While the term 'alienation' can be traced back to thinkers like Rousseau and Hegel (Jaeggi 2014: 6), it is most prominently linked to Marx's theory of capitalist society (ibid: 11). Marx explored how workers become disconnected from the products of their labour, which then exert control over their lives "as something hostile and alien" (Marx 2005 [1844]: 295). As a social relation, the capitalist mode of production, however, not only impacts the connection between workers and their products but also their relationships with themselves and others. While capitalism has evolved since the industrial era, the concept of alienation still remains pertinent today due to the enduring divide between those who control the means of production and those who have only their labour power to sell.

Yet, as many scholars have pointed out, Marx does not offer us a theory of how alienation structurally interlinks with experiences of oppression (Fanon 1952; Said 1978; hooks 1984; Hall 1986; Spivak 1988; Crenshaw 1989; Federici 2004; Fraser 2014; Faye 2021; Gleeson/O'Rourke 2021; among others). To make Marx applicable for my reading of *Fleisch mit weißer Soße*, I will first provide an overview of his conceptualisation of alienation. I then incorporate Rahel Jaeggi's contemporary reinterpretation, which sheds light on alienation as an inherent part of human existence, with individuals continuously shifting between losing and (re)gaining control over their lives.

Through an analysis of Schmacht's text, my aim is to reframe alienation as a lived experience shaped by oppression. I argue that there is a sort of alienation which uniquely impacts trans individuals due to the oppressive constraints of a cisheteronormative framework of gender. I assert that the lens of alienation provides an effective approach to reading trans literature and also a powerful method for literary analysis from a trans-Marxist[1] perspective.

2. Alienation from Marx (1844) to Jaeggi (2014)

The term alienation has a long philosophical history both within Marxist and non-Marxist literature. Offering a genealogy and comprehensive analysis is not the purpose of my analysis.[2] Instead, I will reflect on whether we can make

---

[1] I build here on more recent attempts to articulate a trans-Marxist theory. See, for example, Jules Joanne Gleeson and Elle O'Rourke's *Transgender Marxism* (2021) and Lia Becker's article "Schnitte durch die zweite Haut" (2022).
[2] I would refer interested readers to Jaeggi's chapter titled "A Short History of the Theory of Alienation", where she traces the origins of the term back to Rousseau (Jaeggi 2014: 6–10).

Marx's concept of alienation fruitful for a reading of the experiences of trans (sex) workers under capitalism.

Marx introduces the term alienation in his *Economic and Philosophic Manuscripts* written in 1844, published in 1932, taking it up from his bourgeois predecessors, but expanding it to include the aspect of estranged labour. By highlighting class as the central social relationship, Marx underscores the historically specific exchange-mediated structure of capitalist society which consists in the generalisation of the commodity form. Understanding alienation as a social phenomenon that stems from this specific organisation of society, Marx distinguishes between: 1. alienation from the product of labour – workers no longer have any relation to the product of their work; 2. alienation from the process of production – work no longer represents the satisfaction of a need, but instead turns into 'estranged labour'; 3. alienation of people from their 'species-being' (*Gattungswesen*)[3] which lies in the self-determined processing of the material world; 4. alienation from one another – each person evaluates and perceives others based on commodified terms (cf. Marx 2005: 297–300). Marx's theory of alienation, however, should not be misread as a moralistic critique of capitalist society. He does not suggest that we should return to some former, unalienated state of being, an anthropological constant of sorts. Rather, his account of alienation is to be understood dialectically in that it suggests that alienation can also hold an emancipatory potential if workers become collectively organised as a political subject to reappropriate the products of their labour.

While Marx does not systematically explore the affective dimension of capitalism, his thoughts on alienation do touch upon aspects of the worker's affective experience. For instance, he describes how in the context of estranged labour the worker "does not affirm himself but denies himself, *does not feel content but unhappy*, does not develop freely his physical and mental energy but mortifies his body and ruins his mind" (ibid: 297; my emphasis). This affective dimension makes alienation an apt subject for literary analysis as, in literature, the affective undercurrents of alienation can both be depicted in a nuanced way

---

3   Marx's species-being is characterised by the performance of non-alienated labour as a self-determined, conscious activity, "free from physical need" and "in accordance with the laws of beauty" (Marx 2005: 299–300). In this understanding, the process of actively interacting with and shaping inorganic matter to create objects is central to defining the essence of human beings, but estranged labour reduces "man's species-life" to a mere "means to his physical existence" (ibid. 300).

and brought to resonate with the reader. As literary characters contend with feelings of alienation, they become relatable as embodied, socially interconnected and acting entities. Literature enables us to perceive socially mediated alienation from an individual's perspective and thus sheds light on the interconnection of the individual and the social.

Accordingly, Jaeggi understands alienation as a ruptured relation of the self to the world, a disruption of our capacity to appropriate and act in the world (cf. Jaeggi 2014: 1–2). While drawing on Marx's understanding that "alienation from the world implies alienation from oneself" (ibid: xxi), Jaeggi defines alienation as "a relation of relationlessness" (ibid: 1) which does not consist in "the absence of a relation but is itself a relation, if a deficient one" (ibid.). When feeling alienated, relations with oneself and others still exist, but they lack or significantly diminish the sense of relatedness and connection, identification, belonging or agency.

Rejecting both the widespread idea that alienation entails a lost essence of being human that needs to be regained[4] and the equally common notion that the opposite of alienation is reconciliation or a "unity free of tension" (ibid: 2), Jaeggi suggests that alienation can best be understood in relation to the term "appropriation". Appropriation refers to an ongoing process in which the subject is able to actively and productively engage with its existence, interpersonal connections and the world by integrating and transforming that which is given (ibid: 1). The opposite of alienation would then be the capacity to "*establish[...] relations* to oneself and to the relationships in which one lives" (ibid: 33; emphasis in original). It is, Jaeggi stresses, "a certain way of *carrying out* one's own life and a certain way of *appropriating oneself*" (ibid.).

However, for those facing oppression that goes beyond their status as workers, the act of (self-)appropriation may prove even more difficult. Although Jaeggi does conceptualise alienation as a "relation of domination" (ibid: 22) and problematises the constraining effects of social "conventions"

---

4   Marx's critique that capitalism inhibits the realisation of a certain species-being has given rise to conservative, humanist, anthropological and/or ahistorical interpretations which "emphasize the loss of connection to a given meaningful order" (Jaeggi 2014: 23). Bourgeois philosophy therefore tends to draw on the young Marx to criticise 'immoral' social conditions while at the same time disconnecting him from the idea of class struggle and the necessity of revolution against bourgeois class society.

(ibid: 67),[5] her analysis, like Marx's, does not explicitly address the intersecting experiences of oppressive structures. Yet, I argue that trans individuals face a distinct rupture in their relationship with themselves and the world within a capitalist society which is not only based on the commodity form but simultaneously deeply entrenched in a cisheteronormative matrix of gender. The demand to conform to a binary gender presentation according to one's gender assigned at birth often leads trans individuals to feelings of heightened self-consciousness, worries about external perception and rejection, insecurity, isolation, anxiety, bodily hyper-awareness, and exhaustion from the constant need to explain and justify oneself.

As "distress [...] stemming from the incongruence between experienced gender identity and the sex assigned at birth" (Coleman et al. 2022: 59), these affective phenomena are often referred to as *Gender Dysphoria*. While replacing the term *Gender Identity Disorder* (DSM-5), *Gender Dysphoria* still retains a diagnostic framework that pathologises transness as a psychopathological disorder needing cure. Moreover, these terms primarily attribute the origin of the experienced distress and the responsibility to solve this distress to the individual. In reframing these experiences as manifestations of a ruptured relation to the self and the world, my intention is to understand transness from a structural, contextualised perspective as "a lived engagement with relations of violence and power" (Becker 2022).[6] In my analysis of *Fleisch mit weißer Soße*, I reconsider these lived experiences as negotiations of alienation, focusing on forces that amplify or alleviate it and exploring strategies for addressing it.

3. Alienation in *Fleisch mit weißer Soße*

The narrative opens by depicting a lack of agency in the face of something relatively ordinary. Chrissy wakes up from a nightmare and becomes aware of a rustling sound in his room. Not being able to find the source of the rustling, he retreats into the guest room for the rest of the night. When coming back the next morning, he feels totally overwhelmed and conflicted by the thought that a moth could have died in his room: "I lie on the bed and contemplate – a moth

---

5   While rightly considering conventions as "(normalizing) influence" (Jaeggi 2014: 67), Jaeggi, peculiarly, only mentions childcare and marriage as examples without addressing broader societal conventions like heterosexuality or cisgenderedness.

6   All translations of Becker 2022 are made by the author.

has died in my room. I was lying there. I did not want it to die. But i didn't want it to rustle in my room either" (Schmacht 2017: 4; my translation[7]). The rustling sound serves as a reminder of the persistent presence of external factors that affect Chrissy's life, reinforcing his feelings of being overwhelmed and unable to act. The conflicting emotions Chrissy experiences – not wanting the moth to die but also not wanting it to disturb his personal space – underscore his internal struggle to reconcile his desires with the realities of the situation. The situation described conveys a sense of powerlessness and the feeling that life is happening to him beyond his control.

In the subsequent chapters, it becomes clear that Chrissy feels alienated from everything and from almost everyone. He feels alienated from his work, his family of origin, his friends, his flatmate, his partner and he also feels alienated from the gender assigned to him at birth and his body. The title of the book speaks for itself by pointing towards an objectification of and an alienation from the sex working body, which appears as mere meat, garnished with white sauce as a metaphor for sperm. Although seemingly being able to employ a healthy sense of detachment from his wage labour, Chrissy experiences alienation both from the product and from the process of his work. While working, Chrissy's mind drifts away, rendering him mentally absent: "I go to work, lie under a guy, but think of a colleague who has just told me about the violence she has experienced. She is tender, smart and loving" (ibid: 54). Chrissy also feels alienated from his coworkers and customers, mostly because of their political mindsets ("They are pleased with the afd's result" (ibid: 15)) or intrusive cisheteronormative questions ("Are you into men or women?" (ibid: 4)). But he also feels alienated from those coworkers with whom he could possibly have a better connection, since one is trans and the other one a leftist, but instead "I talk and talk, but skyler doesn't understand me. Nor does franka" (ibid: 69).

When Chrissy goes to work, he continually has to (re-)transform his testosterone induced body "from a hairy queer something into the soft curves of a money maker" (ibid: 9). He faces the pressure and discomfort of having to remove ever more hair from his body (ibid: 49): "I have to shave all over my body.

---

7   *Fleisch mit weißer Soße* was published in 2017 in German, with no English translation available yet. The title could be translated to English as *Meat with White Sauce*. All subsequent quotations of the text are translated to English by the author. In my translations, I aimed to retain the consistent use of lowercase letters as found in the original German, including words like 'i' and people's names.

I hate it" (ibid: 9). In the context of his work, he is annoyed by the cisheteronormative expectations directed towards his body and the cisheterosexual white gaze by which his body is interpreted and assessed, and which does not correspond to his self-image:

> How I see my body is different from how others see it. My body remains invisible when they talk about the body i present to them. They talk about pure, white skin, snow white, the witch or the seductress; they love natural beauty and very specific parts of the body. I look at the ceiling and count the money. (ibid: 19–20)

Chrissy describes a gap between 'my body' and the 'presented body'. The 'presented body' is there for others to project their fantasies on within a racist and cisheterosexist meat market. It is "a satisfaction machine for friends and strangers" (ibid: 18). 'My body', in turn, refers to Chrissy's queer body, which remains invisible. But as a politically educated subject, who knows about the alienating effects of capitalism, patriarchy, racism, etc., Chrissy takes a pragmatic approach towards bodily commodification. He owes to 'his body' that it is able to present itself as 'a body', as material on a meat market, and understands his body as a means "to make money" (ibid: 5) in a society where "our bodies do not belong to us" (ibid: 10). Therefore, Chrissy does not expect life as a trans sex worker under capitalism to be anything other than alienating: "I do not feel indignation, because I am a materialist" (ibid: 45). His work, instead, provides him with time and money to spend on other projects: "Only thanks to the brothel I have the time to write. The time to think. The time and the energy to organise" (ibid: 72). After all, he does not see a more efficient way to earn money: "I don't want to do a job that is more strenuous than this one and pays less" (ibid: 21). Chrissy even tries to form a union once, but the project is quickly dropped because his coworker fears being fired.

Neither romanticising nor demonising sex work, Chrissy highlights the economic reasons behind his engagement. He embraces a feminist-Marxist perspective that regards sex work as work and acknowledges it as an "actively chosen preference to other forms of employment" (O'Connell Davidson 2014: 519). Likewise, Molly Smith and Juno Mac point out that "people sell sex to get money. This simple fact is often missed, forgotten, or overlooked" (Smith/Mac 2020: 46).

While acknowledging sex work as a profession in need of reasonable working conditions, it's still distinctively stigmatised and highly gendered work, making sex workers especially vulnerable to capitalist exploitation. Chrissy's experiences reflect these intersections of capitalism and gender, particularly through the process of feminisation:

> In the brothel, i introduce myself. Again and again, a hundred times, like growing up as a girl in fast forward, day, night, day, night, door opens, hi, a smile, leonie, hello, a flutter of the eyes, my hand, coquetry, shyness. (Schmacht 2017: 15)

It becomes evident that Chrissy sells femininity, yet this paragraph also underscores the temporal, highly repetitive nature of his work. On the one hand, time and temporality are crucial for Chrissy's narrative as he is trying to reconcile gender transition with the capitalist temporality of embodied commodities. Transitioning towards a more masculine body while presenting himself as feminine at the same time, forces Chrissy to negotiate a fundamental contradiction.[8] Right at the beginning, Chrissy states that he "*still* has a body with which to make money" (ibid: 5; my emphasis). At another moment, Chrissy is wondering: "Who knows how much longer i can play this double game here. Passing – i refuse to think about that" (ibid: 21). Chrissy and Skyler, torn between the pressure to market their physical appearance and their desires to transition, assume that they "only carry around passably marketable bodies with the help of [their] underwear" (ibid: 77).

On the other hand, Chrissy emphasises the uniformity of capitalist labour: "The temperature is always the same. The light is always the same. The music is always the same. Everything is always the same. Time stands still […] because every day is the same. All days are the same. The farm of the days, some are more equal" (ibid: 61). In *Capital Vol. 1*, Marx emphasizes that a significant factor contributing to alienation is that "constant labour of one uniform kind disturbs the intensity and flow of a man's animal spirits, which find recreation and delight in mere change of activity" (Marx 1996 [1867]: 346). By creating an environment devoid of meaning, capitalist labour appears intricately linked to depression. Remarkably, however, the text's twelve chapters follow a chronological

---

8   The feeling of contradictoriness is continuously expressed throughout the text, for example, when Chrissy says "I am tired and awake at the same time" (ibid: 95) or when there is "dirt, even if freshly cleaned" (ibid: 8). This means that here, an understanding of capitalism is embraced, which interprets it as an experience of tension, ambiguity, and contradiction.

structure based on months, countering capitalist timelessness with chronology. Chrissy claims that "through writing, i have the illusion of being able to bring the flow of time under my control" (Schmacht 2017: 60). He imposes a structure of time onto his writing to safeguard his sense of time from slipping away, ultimately facilitating self-preservation by reconnecting him with social life.

Although *Fleisch mit weißer Soße* does not appear as a typical trans narrative, the motif of the wrong body is certainly present: "My body: In the bathtub i think, please cut off my breasts, i think, don't listen to my voice, it's a joke. I want to be different, i was born in the wrong body, etc." (ibid: 55). Chrissy finds it challenging to see himself in photos or in the mirror (ibid: 50) and feels sad when thinking about his body (ibid: 62). At one moment, he even wishes to get back to "when it didn't matter – who i am, how others see me" (ibid: 48). The topos of the mirror addresses the optical dimension and the gaze, following Jean-Paul Sartre's conceptualisations of 'the look' (Sartre 2018 [1943]: 347–408). The gazes both of others and himself significantly hinder Chrissy from feeling comfortable, as these gazes make him aware of his body and his being, exerting an objectifying and expropriating influence. Being seen, Sartre explains, is "the alienation of myself" and "implies the alienation of the world I am organizing" (ibid: 360–361). But equally, Chrissy grapples with a feeling of not being seen and recognized. This is evident when his coworker Selina assumes people are attracted to either men or women, or at most both, without considering other spectra of desire. Similarly, when the brothel owner opens the door to a masculine presenting Chrissy, while rationalising him back into womanhood (ibid: 74). Or when the customer Jürgen offers Leonie/Chrissy a career in film and they decline because "the real reason, not working as an actress, however, is that i am not a woman, but a man, but would probably not be cast for a male role" (ibid: 32).

Chrissy is literally illegible to others because they cannot recognise and therefore cannot acknowledge him. But rather than "gaining a sense of intelligibility by virtue of norms" (Butler 2004: 3), Chrissy seems to prefer a strategy of estrangement and social withdrawal. Through the continuous experience of misrecognition, however, Chrissy distances himself from the world which impairs his sense of belonging (cf. ibid.). No wonder, Chrissy feels sick and depressed (ibid: 5), empty (ibid: 6), in pain (ibid: 7), suffers from migraine (ibid: 9), does not sleep or eat (ibid: 18), or, at least, is "thankful and sad at the same time" (ibid: 22).

4. The Text's Body – Schmacht's Autofiction

Alienation is not only a popular topic of modern philosophy, but also a common aesthetic theme in literature. Most prominently, we can think of Dada and the Surrealists, Beckett's, Kafka's and Brecht's aesthetics, Sartre's *La Nausée* (1938), Camus's *L'Étranger* (1942), or Ramón del Valle-Inclan's concept of *Esperpento* as an aesthetics of distortion, first developed in his play *Luces de Bohemia* (1924). The Russian formalist Victor Shklovsky considers alienation, or estrangement, "the most vital capacity of art" (quoted from Dickson 2021: 206). Art is able to change the reader's perception of the everyday, estrange it and let the observer/reader see reality differently. Therefore, Dickson conceives estrangement – both in the context of art and gender transition – as a potential to form new relations with the world and thus for social change (ibid: 207).

Fleisch mit weißer Soße intertextually refers to other works of literature. For Chrissy, a source of connection lies in the solace found through reading literature: "Christa wolf carries me a little way through the fear. You hold my hand, most of the time" (Schmacht 2017: 14). Another time, literature becomes a medium of mutual recognition:

> For the first time i read schernikau[9] and am electrified – is he like me? Does he understand me? Am i like him? Are there more of our kind? But he is dead and even his writing has not stopped the malignant course of the steamroller of capitalism. He says: What does the revolutionary artist do without the revolution? Well, art. [...] I had to become 28 to know that this author existed, who died of aids at 31, who is a look into the mirror and into the future and into the past. I exist! Proof: he existed. (ibid: 41–42)

Chrissy reflects on his own process of writing as allowing him to take a necessary distance, while at the same time intensifying his presence in the world: "I observe and that feels like more than life when you are in the middle of it" (ibid: 60). Ultimately, writing serves him as a counteragent against being silenced:

> Lies that portray our lives differently than they really are are, after all, the instruments of patriarchy; I must somehow confront them SOMEWHERE BUT

---

[9] Schmacht's use of lowercase letters might be influenced by the gay communist writer Ronald M. Schernikau who became famous with his book *Kleinstadtnovelle* (1980).

HOW can i counter them? Tell my story, because whose else, relate it to the story of others. (ibid: 24)

The paratext labels *Fleisch mit weißer Soße* as an 'autobiographically inspired novella'. Due to its lack of clear fictional markers and its appearance as 'authentic', it initially prompts readers to establish an autobiographical pact of truthfulness (cf. Lejeune 1975). However, the main fictionalisation resides in the author's name itself, unveiled as a pseudonym by the German magazine *Der Spiegel* (2019).[10] By employing rhyming invocation and estrangement, the pseudonym takes on added significance as it establishes a parodic reference to the name of the well-known cis-male German contemporary author, Christian Kracht. Similar to a drag name, Schmacht constructs an authorial persona that simultaneously alludes to and questions the relationship between originality and imitation for the context of authorship and authorial enunciation. By invoking Kracht, Schmacht acquires authorial voice and inscribes himself into a German literary discourse.[11]

Using a pseudonym, however, is also a common practice in sex work to ensure privacy. Moreover, in light of the "excessive industry obsession with 'authentic' trans stories and figures" (Mozer 2020: 18), writing 'authentically' as a trans sex worker would require disclosing private information and fostering immediacy and intimacy with one's readers. Schmacht, however, rejects the readers' desire for a 'true story' of a trans sex worker and instead highlights the challenges faced by marginalised individuals when sharing personal experiences in public. The challenge of speaking publicly as a trans sex worker and embodying authorship becomes especially evident when Chrissy compares himself to Jacqueline Frances, a cis, white stripper, which, according to Chrissy, puts her in "the more respectable corner of the industry" (Schmacht 2017: 64). The observation that Frances can promote her books with her face and her body (ibid.) and "can tell a story that is tangible and comprehensible

---

10 This article, published on August 5th, 2019, in *Der Spiegel* was authored by Schmacht himself. Previously, Schmacht had also already been known as the author of a perennial column about sex work in the German pop feminist magazine *Missy Magazine*.

11 It could be argued that by depicting the experiences of a trans man, Schmacht introduces another marginalized form of masculinity to the non-hegemonic masculinities present throughout Kracht's body of work (cf. Dinger 2021: 291). Akin to Dinger's characterisation of Kracht, Schmacht's enactment of authorship is likewise marked by a mode of reserve, distance, and absence (ibid.: 220). Lastly, the theme of alienation is undoubtedly relevant for much of Kracht's work as well.

for others" (ibid.) makes Chrissy feel "small and invisible" (ibid.). He suspects readers are drawn to his text for "all the dirty details" (ibid: 65) whereas he aims to shield himself from voyeurism. Being a trans sex worker, he refrains from promoting his book with his body, knowing that others perceive it differently than he does (ibid: 19). In opting for Christian Schmacht as the name of an authorial persona without public appearance, Schmacht chooses to deprive his readers of an author's body altogether. Instead of a physical presence revealing gender cues, there is only the text, but no body to be read for gender.[12] The withdrawal of the author's body can thus be seen as an opposing response to the expectation to embody authorship in a binarily gendered manner as well as to the particular experience of consistently being embodied as both a transgender and sex working subject.

In this manner, *Fleisch mit weißer Soße* highlights the factual while rejecting authenticity and intimacy. The use of a pseudonym functions as a strategic form of estrangement and self-multiplication, allowing the writer to retain control over the text, avoid exposure and resist the commodification of a marginalised experience for the pleasure of voyeuristic readers. Feeling too vulnerable to engage in an autobiographical discourse of truthfulness, the autofictional, in turn, becomes a textual shelter to explore (in)visibility by offering a protective barrier against exposure, objectification and exoticisation.

5. Existence

By consistently emphasising the term 'existence', Chrissy expresses his determination to resist societal erasure and affirm himself in the text: "I feel like telling stories because I feel like existing" (ibid: 65). The practice of writing and the practice of existing become fundamentally intertwined, making writing a form of existing: "As long as i write, i prove to myself that i exist, that i am complete, not a satisfaction machine for friends and strangers" (ibid: 18).

A central tension in Chrissy's narrative is his desire for relatability, especially when he compares himself to Frances. He laments not feeling as relat-

---

12 Yet, there is a body, or rather two, to be seen on the cover of the book. It is the duplication of the same human being who is wearing a wig, long nails, lipstick and 'feminine' underwear one time, a binder, shaved hair, a 'masculine' necklace, 'masculine' underwear and money the other. It might be tempting to assume that this individual is the author, but without confirmatory paratextual information it remains unclear.

able as Frances but simultaneously claims to write solely for self-preservation: "I write for myself because i want to and sometimes because i have to; to uphold myself. Or to hold" (ibid: 16). The verb 'to relate', however, encompasses both establishing a connection and providing an account. While his main intention for writing is supposedly self-directed, Chrissy, by giving an account of his existence, may still hope that his readers can relate to him, much as he did with Schernikau. This hope suggests that writing and publishing inherently carry an element of relatability, which, in turn, bears the potential to acknowledge and affirm one another's existence through reading.

However, Chrissy's narrative clearly demonstrates the challenges of existing and relating as a trans person within a cisheteropatriarchal capitalist society. Drawing on Sara Ahmed (2016), Lia Becker speaks of transphobia acting "like a permanent hammering that makes the self fragile" (Becker 2022) and considers that "'[n]ot to be housed by gender, to be homeless through gender' (Ahmed 2021, 158) makes it necessary to fight, to insist on one's existence, to be persistent" (Becker 2022). Chrissy persists in his being by writing and insisting on his existence on the page. His act of writing becomes a form of resistance against the alienating forces of cisheteropatriarchal capitalism, involving shared emotional processing and mutual affirmation of existence as essential for connecting with others. After nearly a year, he feels less fatigued and experiences moments of happiness (Schmacht 2017: 76). In the final chapter, he even starts a promising friendship with Melli (ibid: 90). But while ending on a positive note, *Fleisch mit weißer Soße* does not conform to a neoliberal narrative of overcoming depression (cf. Davis 2013: 66) or triumphing over alienation. Instead, it provides a nuanced exploration of a trans sex worker's experiences in capitalism which encourages readers to reflect on the significance of mutual affirmation, care and collective resistance against structural oppression.

6. Conclusions – Owning Gender

In a capitalist society, establishing connections and owning one's life can prove to be challenging and, may at times seem outright impossible. Nevertheless, these connections are vital for political organisation. *Fleisch mit weißer Soße* reflects a yearning for both interpersonal connections and broader social and economic transformations. By acknowledging and articulating the experience of alienation in the act of reading and writing, Chrissy reclaims a sense of existence and belonging.

In terms of gender, Chrissy experiences dysphoria when he is addressed as female while working as Leonie. Turning to Jaeggi, however, makes it possible to read Chrissy's alienation as the result of living within various systems of oppression – economic, social and epistemological – that hinder the unfolding, livability and flourishing of transness, femininity and gender nonconformity. Chrissy's choice to embody Leonie during work hours is a pragmatic strategy to navigate the need to make a living. Similarly, the choice to embody the authorial persona Christian Schmacht is a strategic choice to navigate the expectations of a capitalist book market directed towards trans sex workers to speak intimately about themselves. The embodiment of multiple names and personas thus mirrors the complexity of gender, which does not fit into a binary heteronormative capitalist framework of unambiguity.

With Jaeggi, the process of gender transition itself can be understood as a negotiation of alienation by departing from the gender assigned at birth and appropriating another. "The concept of alienation," Jaeggi says, "concerns itself with the complex conditions of 'linking' one's actions and desires (or, more generally, one's life) with oneself, 'counting them as due to' oneself, or making them *'one's own'*" (Jaeggi 2014: 35; my emphasis). Applying Jaeggi's perspective on transness, the process of transitioning is not seen as the discovery and pursuit of an inner truth; instead, it can be viewed as a response to a profound sense of alienation combined with a desire to transform that which is given to make one's gender one's own.

At the same time, Butler reminds us that "what I call my 'own' gender appears perhaps at times as something that I author or, indeed, own. But the terms that make up one's own gender are, from the start, outside oneself, beyond oneself in a sociality that has no single author" (Butler 2004: 1). Consequently, as "one does not 'do' one's gender alone" (ibid.), gender cannot be a fixed or given identity, but is an ongoing process and a shared exploration of self-presentation and realisation with others. Reading trans narratives through the lens of alienation reveals gender transitions as "an embodied, pleasurable and painful, contradictory *work* of *unlearning hegemonic and appropriating* new ways of thinking, feeling and acting" (Becker 2022; emphasis of 'work' in original, rest mine).

In the past, trans people predominantly shared their stories through autobiographical accounts, often referred to as 'body narratives', as Jay Prosser described these accounts due to their focus on "stories of bodies in sex transition" (Prosser 1998: 4). Prosser argued that narrative is essential for healing "the rupture in gendered plots" (ibid: 9). In a deliberate departure from the conventional transition narrative, *Fleisch mit weißer Soße* blurs the boundaries between autobiography and fiction while inhabiting differently gendered personas. Nonetheless, it remains a body narrative by resolutely addressing the challenges of trans embodiment. Similar to autofiction's blend of autobiography and fiction, Chrissy skilfully navigates different embodiments, purposefully inviting differently gendered pacts of reading. By taking authorship of both his narrative and his body, Chrissy embraces and claims the multiplicity of gendered embodiment. When he goes out with friends in wigs and "slutty schoolgirl costumes" (Schmacht 2017: 104), he taps into "the power that drag can bestow" (ibid.) and feels "alive, unpredictable, strong" (ibid: 105). Chrissy not only embraces the embodiment of multiple genders, but also explores femininity as a trans man, reflecting a desire to exist in complexity.

Consequently, Schmacht does not portray transness as a rupture in gendered plots in need of healing. Instead, the text succeeds in depicting Chrissy's complex relationship with his body within a capitalist cisheteropatriarchal society. The split that Chrissy encounters is not between different genders nor embodiments but rather between normative and nonnormative ways of living gender and desire, between the marginalised and the norm, between visibility and invisibility, between workers and capitalists. Through autofiction, Schmacht's body narrative does not heal a rupture in gendered plots but embraces this rupture in order to challenge forms of domination in contemporary capitalism.

References

Ahmed, Sara (2016): "An Affinity of Hammers." In: TSQ Transgender Studies Quarterly 3/1-2, pp. 22–34.
Ahmed, Sara (2021 [2017]): Feministisch leben! Manifest für Spaßverderberinnen, Münster: Unrast.
Becker, Lia (2022): "Schnitte durch die zweite Haut Über Gender-Gewalt und Heilung, Klasse und trans*feministische Allianzen." In: Luxemburg. Gesellschaftsanalyse und linke Praxis, June 06, 2023 (https://zeitschrift-luxemburg.de/artikel/schnitte-durch-die-zweite-haut/).
Butler, Judith (2004): Undoing Gender, New York and London: Routledge.
Coleman, E. et al. (2022): "Standards of Care for the Health of Transgender and Gender Diverse People, Version 8." In: International Journal of Transgen-

der Health 23/1, pp. 1–258, https://doi.org/10.1080/26895269.2022.2100644.

Crenshaw, Kimberlé (1989): "Demarginalizing the Intersection of Race and Sex: A Black Feminist Critique of Antidiscrimination Doctrine, Feminist Theory and Antiracist Politics." In: University of Chicago Legal Forum 1/8, pp. 139–167.

Davis, Lennard J. (2013): The End of Normal. Identity in a Biocultural Era, Ann Arbor: University of Michigan Press.

Dickson, Nathaniel (2021): "Seizing the Means: Towards a Trans Epistemology." In: Jules Joanne Gleeson/Elle O'Rourke (eds.), Transgender Marxism, London: Pluto Press, pp. 204–218.

Dinger, Christian (2021): Die Aura des Authentischen. Inszenierung und Zuschreibung von Authentizität auf dem Feld der deutschsprachigen Gegenwartsliteratur, Göttingen: Vandenhoeck & Ruprecht.

Fanon, Frantz (2008 [1952]): Black Skin, White Masks, London: Pluto Press.

Faye, Shon (2021): The Transgender Issue. An Argument for Justice, London: Allen Lane.

Federici, Silvia (2004): Caliban and the Witch. Women, the Body and Primitive Accumulation, Williamsburg: Autonomedia.

Fraser, Nancy (2014): "Behind Marx's Hidden Abode: For an Expanded Conception of Capitalism." In: New Left Review 86 (https://newleftreview.org/issues/ii86/articles/nancy-fraser-behind-marx-s-hidden-abode).

Gleeson, Jules Joanne/O'Rourke, Elle (eds.) (2021): Transgender Marxism, London: Pluto Press.

Hall, Stuart (1986): "Gramsci's Relevance for the Study of Race and Ethnicity." In: Journal of Communication Inquiry 10/2 (https://doi.org/10.1177/019685998601000202).

hooks, bell (1984): Feminist Theory: From Margin to Center, Boston: South End Press.

Jaeggi, Rahel (2014): Alienation, New York: Columbia University Press.

Lejeune, Philippe (1975): Le Pacte Autobiographique, Paris: Seuil.

Marx, Karl (1996 [1867]): "Capital. A Critique of Political Economy. Volume 1." In: Karl Marx, Frederick Engels: Collected Works, Vol. 35, Karl Marx: Capital, Vol. 1, New York: International Publishers.

Marx, Karl (2005 [1844]): "Economic and Philosophic Manuscripts of 1844." In: Karl Marx, Frederick Engels: Collected Works, Vol. 3, Marx and Engels: 1843–1844, New York: International Publishers, pp. 251–370.

Mozer, Gil (2020): Writing Transgender. Speculative and Real, May 13, 2023 (https://scholarship.miami.edu/esploro/outputs/doctoral/Writing-Transgender-Speculative-and-Real/991031496988902976).

O'Connell Davidson, Julia (2014): "Let's Go Outside: Bodies, Prostitutes, Slaves and Worker Citizens." In: Citizenship Studies, 18/5, pp. 516–532.

Prosser, Jay (1998): Second Skins. The Body Narratives of Transsexuality, New York: Columbia University Press.

Said, Edward W. (1978): Orientalism, New York: Pantheon.

Sartre, Jean-Paul (2018 [1943]): Being and Nothingness. New York and London: Routledge.

Schmacht, Christian (2017): Fleisch mit weißer Soße, Münster: edition assemblage.

Schmacht, Christian (2019): "Ich bin Sexarbeiter – und ihr könnt mir meinen Job nicht verbieten", August 05, 2019 (https://www.spiegel.de/panorama/sexarbeit-warum-prostitution-nicht-kriminalisiert-gehoert-a-ff7fcfc8-bd9a-49e3-9af7-0b2ddde77517).

Schmacht, Christian (2021): "Ich höre auf mit Christian Schmacht." In: Missy Magazine, November 16, 2021 (https://missy-magazine.de/blog/2021/11/16/ich-hoere-auf-mit-christian-schmacht/).

Smith, Molly/Mac, Juno (2020): Revolting Prostitutes. London: Verso.

Spivak, Gayatri Chakravorty (1988): "Can the Subaltern Speak?" In: Cary Nelson/Lawrence Grossberg (eds.), Marxism and the Interpretation of Culture, Basingstoke: Macmillan, pp. 271–313.

Affective Becoming, Affective Belonging: A Queer Phenomenological Account of the Social Reproduction of Bodies

Jannis Ruhnau

> To prevent possible misunderstanding, a word. I paint the capitalist and the landlord in no sense *couleur de rose*. But here individuals are dealt with only in so far as they are the personifications of economic categories, embodiments of particular class relations and class interests. My standpoint, from which the evolution of the economic formation of society is viewed as a process of natural history, can less than any other make the individual responsible for relations whose creature he socially remains, however much he may subjectively raise himself above them. (Marx 2010 [1867]: 10)

In his preface to the first German edition of *Capital*, Karl Marx emphasises that he deals with individuals living in capitalist society only as embodiments of specific social relations. He abstracts from the concrete to develop his theory of capitalism. This allows us to understand the capitalist mode of production and structural organisation of society, but leaves us with few tools to make sense of how we as individuals experience this society apart from being personifications of economic social relations. Many scholars and activists have broadened Marx's theoretical framework (cf. Skeggs et al. 2019; Gleeson/O'Rourke 2021); nevertheless it remains difficult to include the living individual in Marxist perspectives. The individual story only comes to fit into Marxist categories when individuals begin to organise (cf. Thompson 2021). In my own research, whenever I try to apply Marxist thinking to what phenomenology considers the "systematic description of first-person experience" (Haulotte 2023: 32), I struggle not to fall into dualistic notions, which place individuals as either privileged or unprivileged, discriminated or not discriminated against, radical or normative.

When Marx says he only considers individuals as embodiments of capitalist social relations, we might wonder: how do individuals experience these embodiments? As Søren Mau writes in his article on "The Body" (2019) in Marxist thought, perspectives on the body have been rare, although Marx himself considers the body in his writings, for example when he ponders how bodies are shaped by rhythms of production (cf. ibid: 1272). In this article, I show how bodies are not only shaped by these rhythms but also by modes of social reproduction and the need for care and affirmation. This is by no means a new argument, but by working with life stories in narrative interviews, I analyse how bodily surfaces are produced in affective relations between spaces, objects and other bodies, which can dis/enable individuals to reproduce their own existence. I will do so, first, by revisiting Sara Ahmed's queer phenomenological account of affective becoming, and, second, by combining it with Zoe Belinsky's perspective on how bodies can only become labouring bodies through reproductive work. Through this phenomenological-Marxist account, I finally analyse insights from an interview I conducted in Spring 2022.

1. Queer Phenomenology and Marxism?

1.1 Histories of Contact: Ahmed's Queer Phenomenologist Approach

In her *Queer Phenomenology* Sara Ahmed seeks to incorporate a Marxist perspective into her phenomenological approach. In her critique of traditional phenomenologists like Edmund Husserl and Maurice Merleau-Ponty, she argues that phenomenology cuts off its object of interest and inquiry from its own arrival by only taking into consideration what can be perceived at a present moment. This perspective misses the background and historical becoming of an object, its past directions and interactions, which made it possible for the object to appear at a certain place in a certain time (cf. Ahmed 2006: 2). She builds her argumentation on Marx' understanding of commodity fetishism, which accentuates the histories of objects:

> Insofar as Marxism emphasizes the disappearance of labor in commodity fetishism, then it too provides a model of history as disappearance. A queer phenomenology, in which phenomenology is in dialogue with psychoanalysis and Marxism, might go 'behind the back' to account for what disappears in how things appear. (ibid: 190)

Ahmed uses this perspective to sketch out how objects, bodies and spaces are co-constitutive: "Neither the object nor the body have integrity in the sense of being 'the same thing' with and without others." (ibid: 54) Instead of perceiving bodies, objects and spaces as entities in themselves, Ahmed points to how they are intertwined. Spaces are shaped by the bodies and objects assembled inside them and vice versa. Ahmed emphasises that "some spaces extend certain bodies and simply do not leave room for others" (ibid: 11). For example: "When we refer to [...] 'white space' we are talking about the repetition of the passing by of some bodies and not others." (ibid:135) White spaces extend white bodies, even to a point where one will not notice the whiteness of spaces if one is white oneself. Only if our bodies are not extended might we feel the space being full of obstacles, hindering our capacities, positing ourselves in a different place than others (cf. ibid: 132).

Ahmed's perspective enables us to take a look at how embodied individuals are directed through spaces, objects, relations with others as well as through practices they carry out: "in moving this way, rather than that, and moving in this way again and again, the surfaces of bodies in turn acquire their shape. Bodies are 'directed' and they take the shape of this direction." (ibid: 16) Precisely because bodies are not only doing things and encountering objects as being distinct from them, but actually gain their very own shapes during the ongoing contacts throughout life, the directedness is *in* the body and even *is* the body itself. Where individuals go is always accompanied by a history of where they have been going, because some ways and some objects are closer to them than others (cf. ibid: 56, 66). This history is an affective history. During the contact with the world around us we become affected and we feel these affects in our bodies. Our bodies remember these encounters, they leave affective traces and become a part of ourselves. In this way they also structure feelings of belonging and non-belonging: "affects [...] are basically ways of connecting, to others and to other situations [...] With intensified affect comes [...] a heightened sense of belonging, with other people and to other places" (Massumi 2015: 110). To understand how someone arrived at certain places, their affective history of becoming must be taken into consideration.

This interrelatedness of bodies, objects and spaces is usually invisible if one only considers an object as it appears to be in a given moment. Yet, what is actually Marxist about Ahmed's interpretation remains unclear. In fact, she even strips commodity fetishism of its Marxist meaning. Marx accentuates how commodities are perceived as carrying value whereas the production of this value remains hidden. This value production can be considered as the commodity's history, the labour which manufactured it. As individuals exchange commodities on the market, "we equate as values our different products, [and] by that very act, we also equate, as human labour, the different kinds of labour expended upon them" (Marx 2010 [1867]: 84–85). Individuals relate to one another and to themselves in terms of commodity values. These values appear as natural, as belonging to specific products and kinds of work. But:

> The character of having value, when once impressed upon products, obtains fixity only by reason of their acting and reacting upon each other as quantities of value. These quantities vary continually, independently of the will, foresight and action of the producer. To them, their own social action takes the form of the action of objects, which rule the producers instead of being ruled by them. (ibid: 85)

This specific meaning of commodity fetishism is not summed up in the history of the labour put into commodities or objects. It always exceeds this history and points to the specific ruling mechanisms in capitalist society.

Ahmed does, however, show how individuals become directed in their bodies, habits and practices and how these directions remain hidden – call that fetishism or not. I will inform these histories of contacts constituting individual bodies with Zoe Belinsky's social reproduction lens, which combines phenomenological and Marxist thinking in order to understand how individual bodies are enabled and disenabled to labour and reproduce themselves in capitalist society.

1.2 *I Cannot* and *I Can*: Belinsky's Phenomenology of (Reproductive) Work

In her essay "Transgender and Disabled Bodies: Between Pain and the Imaginary" (2021), Zoe Belinsky develops a phenomenological account of the Marxist term *work*. She argues that in order to work, individuals need to transform the nonfoundational experience of an *I cannot* into an *I can*. Like Ahmed, Belinsky rejects the way in which traditional phenomenologists such as Merleau-Ponty generalise their own bodily experience into an ontological experience of individuals. As Merleau-Ponty states that individuals turn towards the world with an attitude of *I can*, Belinsky reveals the male, white and ableist character of this experience (cf. Belinsky 2021: 179, 188). She further argues:

The dialectic of the 'I can' and the 'I cannot' is the phenomenological horizon of the social reproduction of capitalist societies. It is the medium through which the labouring classes individually and collectively experience the reproduction of their existence. (ibid: 187)

In capitalist societies "workers are expected to appear at their workplaces with *their capacities* fully intact" (ibid: 180, original emphasis), but to capacitate themselves individuals must work to overcome the pain which accompanies the experience of the *I cannot*. In this sense "[t]o suffer is to experience the incapacity to remove the object, which causes sensuous pain" (ibid: 187). Belinsky discusses how trans people, people of colour, women, disabled people and other marginalised groups face more difficulties in transforming the incapacitating conditions they experience in their daily lives due to forms of structural discrimination like limited access to health care providers (cf. ibid: 193). In short, reproductive work – necessary to transform the experience of *I cannot* into *I can* – is more difficult for some people than for others.

1.3 Spaces, Bodies, Others: Affective Conditions of Capacitating Oneself and Others

I argue that the dimensions of reproductive work and the conditions, which enable and disenable individuals to reproduce their existence are connected to the constitutions of bodies, objects and spaces. Being dis/enabled to capacitate oneself is connected to how bodies can/not move, which spaces they can/not access, which other bodies are close to them and which objects they can/not reach. I argue that the experiences of *I can* and *I cannot* can be understood analogously to how Ahmed considers that some places extend specific bodies and not others. In this sense experiences of capacitation and incapacitation are connected to specific relations between bodies, spaces and objects. These relations are affective: Belinsky considers the experience of *I cannot* to be an experience of pain and Ahmed remarks that "it is through the flow of sensations and feelings that become conscious as pain and pleasure that different surfaces are established" (Ahmed 2014 [2004]: 24). Experienced and enacted embodiment is thus shaped and guided by affects which come to materialise *in* the body and *as* its skin. We need to "unlearn the assumption that the skin is simply already there, and begin to think of the skin as a surface that is felt only in the event of being 'impressed upon' in the encounters we have with others" (ibid: 25). The antagonistic character of social reproduction in capitalist society and the pain we feel in the experience of *I cannot* unfolds as our skin. It is the bodily manifestation of our inability to reproduce ourselves in capitalist society without selling our labour since the means of reproduction do not belong to us (cf. Lewis 2022 [2016]: xi).

2. Body Shapes in Affective Relations

I will now interweave this perspective with an analysis of a narrative interview I conducted with Amira.[1] As I follow the remarks Ahmed made about taking into consideration the histories of how someone arrives at a certain place, I will trace the different narrative elements Amira told me about herself and the relationship to her body. I understand *bodies* as being physical, historical and social at the same time, rejecting essentialist notions about their characteristics. As Ahmed writes, bodily surfaces are constituted by engaging with the world. The shape of a body varies socially and historically. How individuals feel and see their bodies is mediated through social discourses and images and their personal histories of contacts (cf. Haraway 1994; Morris 2004; Ahmed 2006; Preciado 2016; Haddow 2021).

2.1 Between the Maghreb, France and Germany: Amira's Life Story

My interview with Amira was conducted in early spring 2022. I started the interview by asking her if she could tell me how she felt in her body throughout her life. This evoked a narration of Amira's life story with recurring references to her body. Amira grew up in a small village in France. She speaks French, Arabic, English and some German; the interview was conducted in English. Amira is a qualified engineer. She moved to a large city in France for her master's degree. Her parents are from the Maghreb and immigrated to France, both gaining advanced degrees and building successful careers. Amira has one sister and one brother. During her master's programme she came to realise she was attracted to women and met her first girlfriend, Sarah. She uses the term *gay* for self-identification. Amira was outed to her family by a friend of a cousin, who saw her and Sarah holding hands. Amira calls the events of this outing, leading to a fundamental break between her and her family, "the apocalypse" (Amira, personal communication, 19th March 2022). When Amira refused to

---

[1] All names relating to the interview data have been changed.

break up with Sarah, her parents threatened and pressured her. Being scared, Amira chose to move back and forth between Germany, where Sarah lived, and France to finish her degree. She moved to Germany afterwards, then being in her mid-twenties. Later, Amira and Sarah moved in together and got married during the corona pandemic. They now live in a house they have bought. Amira was in her early thirties when we conducted the interview.

2.2 Medical Stigmatisation: The Emergence of a Felt Body Type

Right at the beginning of our interview Amira states that she had always felt she was "overweight" (ibid). This feeling seems to have been established by early medical records and examinations, which documented her body size as exceeding medical standards from the birth throughout her childhood and puberty. During the interview Amira repeatedly refers to herself as not fitting the norm in terms of body shape and size. She connects this to her desire "to defy expectations" (ibid). Pointing out that in society overweight people are not expected to be sporty. she explains her focus on practising taekwondo during her childhood and puberty, later developing a passion for weightlifting in her mid-twenties. Although Amira displayed pride about having had "the reputation of doing martial arts" (ibid) in school, her relationship to her body has been conflicted ever since she can remember: "I always felt kinda like you know this big, this big thing that you don't know what to do with yourself" (ibid). Her self-consciousness is formed by the medical norms she was exposed to. Although she pointed to their normative character, Amira struggles with the consequences these categorisations imply. As Sabrina Strings has argued in her Book *Fearing the Black Body: The Racial Origins of Fat Phobia* (2019), "the phobia about fatness and the preference for thinness […] have been one way the body has been used to craft and legitimate race, sex, and class hierarchies" (ibid: 6). Strings analyses how fat-phobic discourses shifted over time. In the 18th century black people were increasingly characterised "as greedy eaters" (ibid: 84) and "[i]ndulging in food […] became evidence of actual low breeding" (ibid). Fat phobia is thus deeply entangled with racism and eugenics and the medical system engaged in the construction of these norms by connecting health to body sizes, shapes and skin colour. At the end of the 19th and the beginning of the 20th century medical discourses shifted, focusing less on condemning black bodies and bodies of colour. Instead, discourses explicitly concentrated on the medicalisation of white bodies, serving as the desired norm (cf. ibid: 180). Amira is exposed to this norm of white women, which she will never be able to attain. She is thus confronted with the experience of an *I cannot* which cannot easily be worked upon to remove the object of pain. This form of disenablement – being compared with a norm which is not even allegedly made to be reachable by her – did not remain outside Amira's body, but started to shape its contours early on. Amira felt the stigmatisation *in* her body, for example when she talks about how she doesn't want to be watched while training, because she is aware of the fat-phobic attitudes and gazes she is exposed to. Shame is thus the affective register structuring her perception of her body shape and she states she tried "to dodge thinking about my body, which was the obvious thing that was not correct with me" (Amira, personal communication, 19th March 2022).

2.3 Gender in Different Spaces

This 'dodging' worked until puberty, when people around Amira started dating: "I remember that yeah this is where I knew I felt ugly because, well, no one asked me out" (ibid). Although she did not even want to be asked out, she nevertheless felt the desire to relate to the other kids around her and mimicked their behaviour: "I remember that you know the girls were writing like the names of their boyfriend or of the boys they liked and I would just write a random name so because I didn't understand why I didn't feel that way" (ibid). Although she felt "indifferent to men" (ibid) Amira tried to be part of the practices she observed, but she didn't succeed. This experience led to reflections about gender and ethnicity: "It was always the same types of girls that had boyfriends, it's like the petite ones that already had boobs that were white" (ibid). Amira did not fit this profile: she was neither white nor petite. Additionally, she often wore masculine clothes and hung out with the boys, thus positioning herself in contrast to the girls described. On top of the medical institutions telling her that her body exceeded the norms, the dating experience made her feel she did not fit the norms for the dating game either. This led her to reflect on her gender identity and she went back and forth about "flirting with non-binarity" (ibid) but also wishing that "being strong and tall and bla, to not be gendered qualities" (ibid).

Whereas she wasn't able to share the dating experience in puberty and thus struggled to identify with her peers, fat phobia and gender stereotypes were not relevant in her family. Amira told me that she has never been fat shamed at home and body type and appearance weren't discussed. At the same time, she talked about having "had a vehemently egalitarian education" (ibid). Since both her parents have successful careers and her father supported her mother so that she could go back to university to finish her degrees, Amira considers her parents somewhat feminist: "I don't know whether my parents were really activists in feminism, but I think they kind of are in a way" (ibid). Experiencing an egalitarian education meant for Amira not having been treated differently than her brother and engaging in the same tasks in the household.

It seems as if Amira experienced different allocations and expectations in the spaces she engaged with in her childhood and puberty: at home she felt accepted or at least her body and gender were not subject to conversation. At the doctor's, at school and with her peers she experienced gendered expectations about her body type and comportment, which left her struggling and developing a torn relationship to her body. Although Amira is conscious about the structural dimensions of the normative ideals she is confronted with, we can see how they access her body. The shaping of Amira's bodily surface can be understood as a mixture of normative notions and standards she felt exposed to at the doctor's and at school combined with the egalitarian and unbothered attitude in her family. These traces unfold as her skin. Depending on the spaces she encounters her skin shows marks of irritation or a feeling of belonging. Whereas she is confronted with the experience of *I cannot* in her dating experience and her medical appointments, her family offers her an opportunity to reinstate her capacities by performing all the tasks she wants to and wearing the clothes she likes.

2.4 Loss of the Family and Racist Encounters: Body without Space

This changes when Amira comes to realise she is attracted to women after moving far away from her family's home to a big city to study. After being outed to her family she is pressured and threatened to make her break up with her girlfriend Sarah. Amira lives through pain, grieve and fear, not knowing if her family might come to take her back to their home with them, disenabling her from seeing Sarah. The pain of this disruption seemed to be still present at the time of the interview. Amira was crying, trying to make sense of why her family abandoned her. Especially because she had always experienced them as being liberal due to the education and uprising she experienced, it is difficult for her to grasp the rejection she now undergoes. Amira does not think of her parents as homophobic, but believes that they are punishing her for not fulfilling their expectations: "It's because I didn't listen and when you don't listen it's a social suicide" (Amira, personal communication, 19th March 2022). She went on to tell me that in her culture "the opinion of the group is more important than the individual" (ibid). Salima Amari has shown in her research on lesbians of Maghrebi origin in France that they developed a "strategy for living their affective and sexual life without taking the risk of losing the familial space"[2] (Amari 2013: 218), in order to respond to the felt pressure of their families. This strategy consists of not talking about their sexuality and even denying homo- or bisexuality when it comes to confrontations. Amira seems to be aware of this possibility. She talked about how it was possible to be gay in her culture when people don't talk about it, but she decided not to participate in this strategy of denial. We can thus see that through the rupture with her family – formerly a space where she was able to recharge her capacities and to transform experiences of *I cannot* into *I can* – she was then confronted with a huge disruption, stripping her of a place of belonging and care.

As the rupture with her family caused loss and trauma, Amira tried to find support elsewhere, reaching out to white queer spaces as well as to a white therapist. In both places she was confronted with racial stereotypes about Muslims and their alleged views on gender and sexuality. While she was suffering, white queer spaces and the white healthcare system failed to support her. Even worse, they confronted her with racism, putting her in the position of defending her family. Amira felt as if she "didn't even exist" (Amira, personal communication, 19th March 2022). Once again, she did not fit the expectations and concepts of white hegemonic culture. She emphasised that she

> suffered more from racism than homophobia because at least when I get back home at my parents', people are looking like me they have the same cultural reference. Also they don't question the very existence of racism because they are also suffering from it. (ibid)

Amira was not only losing an important place where she received acceptance and care and had the opportunity to mirror herself in the bodies around her, she was also confronted with white spaces not extending her body, disenabling her from existing in them, leaving her with no space to reside in. This led to a phase of Amira's life in which she described herself as "suicidal" (ibid). Amira told me about how she thought about ending her life but was prevented to do so by Sarah who texted her in the right moment. As I have argued, spaces and bodies co-constitute each other and Amira's story shows how her body nearly

---

2   Translation made by the author.

faded into nonexistence when she lost the space she resided in and was prevented from finding new ones. Her story poses questions about whether bodies can exist without spaces and, in capitalist society, this means spaces of care. Being suicidal must be considered the core of not being able to reproduce one's existence, of not being able to remove the object of pain, where instead the terminating of life itself seems like the only option to escape the incapacitating conditions which render life unliveable.

2.5 Loving and Lifting: New Body Shapes

The trauma and loss Amira experienced accounts for the dark sides of what she lived through while discovering she was gay, meeting her partner and finishing her studies. At the same time these new encounters also allowed her to address herself and her body in new ways and experience love and care directly linked to her body and body shape. While Amira realised she was attracted to women she discovered:

> I want women to be attracted to me in two ways: like in the most like beautiful in the quintessence of femininity that you can imagine in the world, like I want them to find me beautiful just like I want them to find me handsome. The way that they're attracted to men. (ibid)

Coming to terms with her sexuality also made her consolidate different longings concerning her gender identity, making room for what she considers feminine and masculine aspects of herself. She stresses that she wants women to like "those qualities about me I didn't like" (ibid) and finds these desires met in her relationship with Sarah. She tells me about how Sarah would touch her shoulders or her hair, calling her strong and beautiful. These touches reshape Amira's body. According to Amira it was also Sarah who kept her from committing suicide, providing love, care and support.

The reshaping of Amira's body is also enforced by her engaging in strength training: "I feel good when I work out, you know, I feel powerful, high on endorphins" (ibid). She goes on to tell me that she enjoys to touch her shoulders and feel her own strength (cf. ibid). We can see how these feelings concerning her body emerge in new ways of contact, with Sarah as her partner and objects like weight machines enabling Amira to feel herself differently. Instead of the *I cannot* that accompanied her experience in the medical system, at school and later also with her family and in white spaces, she experiences new possibilities, feelings of power and strength. Amira's descriptions of her relationship with Sarah and her relationship to lifting provide an account of how her body comes into a different shape in these relations. Her body, which had been shaped by hegemonic white health and gender discourses, which produced shame, now comes to be felt by her differently: Her broad shoulders in contact with Sarah and lifting weights become strong, and in the way Sarah looks at her, expressing her attraction, Amira feels beautiful.

3. Conclusion: Creating Spaces of Care and Belonging

As I have argued with references to Ahmed and Belinsky, questions of social reproduction and care work come to matter as bodily surfaces and are felt as one's own skin. My analysis of Amira's life story and her history of contacts emphasises that individuals not only experience enabling and disenabling conditions as residing outside of themselves, but that these conditions shape their bodies and are felt in the body. The structural dimensions of the disenabling conditions that Amira was and is experiencing disappear as outside relations and become manifest in her body and as her skin instead. When she met Sarah, Amira's ways of relating to herself and to others started to change. Yet, this also cut her off from spaces in which she felt safe and familiar. While she was able to relate to herself in new ways, transforming her bodily experience from *I cannot* into *I can* by receiving affirming care from her partner and through the practice of strength training, she lost access to her family – a space which no longer extended her body. In her marriage with Sarah, Amira built a new space of love, care and belonging. As I said in the beginning of this article, Amira's life story and bodily becoming does not seem to lend itself in an obvious way to a Marxist perspective. She is not a factory worker of the kind Marx might have pictured at the time of his writings, but has a secure and well-paid job, owns a house and is married. She also did not mention being politically organised, when the interview was conducted. And yet Amira's story and the different shapes of her body are political. They tell a story of surviving in incapacitating circumstances in capitalist society, where the "heterosexual family is one of the central circuits of social reproduction" (Belinsky 2021: 193).

It is important to notice what Amira's story tells us about social reproduction, which concerns the realms of care and love. In her intimate relationship she was able to find the resources to stay alive and reproduce her own existence. By building a marriage, buying a house and pets, Sarah and Amira constituted a space where these resources would flourish, where they could care and watch out for each other. This might remind us at once of the many ways in which romantic relationships are political. In the case of Amira it could provide what she needed to survive. Needless to say, marital and private spaces of social reproduction are important sites of the reproduction of capitalist social relations: "What capitalism relies on is the unpaid reproduction and maintenance of its workforce." (Lewis 2022 [2016]: 116) Amira's attempts to reach out for support elsewhere failed and the white queer groups as well as the white therapist proved to be spaces which reproduced their own whiteness by revoking Amira's experience, disenabling her to reside in them. This shows exactly how individuals who face marginalisation in multiple ways have limited access to the health care system and community services. It should be a reminder that whether individuals are able to politically organise and find spaces in which they can support one another and fight together is highly dependent on the spaces we create and the bodies who gather inside them. It is often stressed that trans and queer people form support networks and provide the care for each other that they are refused by the medical system. Amira's story shows how we must reflect on which bodies are extended by these networks and which are not.

A queer phenomenological perspective enriched with thinking about social reproduction and care work can help to understand how individuals experience the contradictory character of social reproduction in capitalism in and also as their own bodies. Capitalism needs labouring bodies, it needs us to reappear at our workplace every day, rested and in the state of *I can*, and yet it constantly shortens public resources for social reproduction in order to increase surplus value (cf. Raha 2021: 92). My analysis shows that we cannot idealise spaces of care as places of resistance, because they are essential to the reproduction of capitalist society, but that stories like those of Amira are stories of individual survival under capitalist conditions. These conditions differ among labouring individuals, as different aspects of discrimination and marginalisation intersect and produce specific experiences. We need to carefully analyse them and pay attention to the details if we want to get the complete picture of how contemporary capitalism is lived and experienced by its different participants.

References

Ahmed, Sara (2006): Queer Phenomenology, Durham and London: Duke University Press.

Ahmed, Sara (2014 [2004]): The Cultural Politics of Emotion, Edinburgh: Edinburgh University Press.

Amari, Salima (2013): "Sujets Tacites: Le Cas De Lesbiennes D'origine Maghrébine." In: Tumultes 41/2, pp. 205–221.

Belinsky, Zoe (2021): "Transgender and Disabled Bodies: Between Pain and the Imaginary." In: Jules Joanne Gleeson/Elle O'Rourke (eds.), Transgender Marxism, London: Pluto Press, pp. 179–199.

Gleeson, Jules Joanne/O'Rourke, Elle (eds.) (2021): Transgender Marxism, London: Pluto Press.

Haddow, Gill (2021): Embodiment and Everyday Cyborgs, Manchester: Manchester University Press.

Haraway, Donna (1994): "A Manifesto for Cyborgs: Science, Technology, and Socialist Feminism in the 1980s." In: Steven Seidmann (ed.), The Postmodern Turn: New Perspectives on Social Theory, Cambridge: Cambridge University Press, pp. 82–116.

Haulotte, Penelope (2023): "Program for a Transgender Existentialism." In: TSQ: Transgender Studies Quarterly 10/1, pp. 32–41.

Lewis, Holly (2022 [2016]): The Politics of Everybody: Feminism, Queer Theory, and Marxism at the Intersection, London, New York and Dublin: Bloomsbury Academic.

Marx, Karl (2010 [1867]): "Preface of the First German Edition." In: Karl Marx/Friedrich Engels (eds.), Karl Marx, Frederick Engels. Collected Works Volume 35, London: Lawrence & Wishart Electric Book, pp. 7–11.

Massumi, Brian (2015): The Power at the End of the Economy, Durham: Duke University Press.

Mau, Søren (2019): "The Body." In: Beverly Skeggs/Sara R. Farris/Alberto Toscano/Svenja Bromberg (eds.), Sage Handbook of Marxism, London, Thousand Oaks, New Delhi and Singapore: Sage Publications, pp. 1268–1286.

Morris, David (2004): The Sense of Space, Albany: State University of New York Press.

Preciado, Paul B. (2016): Testo Junkie: Sex, Drogen und Biopolitik in der Ära der Pharmapornographie, Berlin: b_books.

Raha, Nat (2021): "A Queer Marxist Transfeminism: Queer and Trans Social Reproduction." In: Jules Joanne Gleeson/Elle O'Rourke (eds.), Transgender Marxism, London: Pluto Press, pp. 85–115.
Skeggs, Beverly/Farris, Sara R./Toscano, Alberto/Bromberg, Svenja (eds.) (2019): Sage Handbook of Marxism, London, Thousand Oaks, New Delhi and Singapore: Sage Publications.
Strings, Sabrina (2019): Fearing the Black Body: The Racial Origins of Fat Phobia, New York: New York University Press.
Thompson, Farah (2021): "The Bridge between Gender and Organising." In: Jules Joanne Gleeson/Elle O'Rourke (eds.), Transgender Marxism, London: Pluto Press, pp. 156–164.

Contributors

Contributors

Edith Otero Quezada is a PhD candidate in InterAmerican Studies and Research Associate at the Interdisciplinary Center for Gender Research (IZG) at the University of Bielefeld. She was a scholarship holder of the Rosa Luxemburg Stiftung (2017–2020). Her research interests are feminist epistemologies, political subjectivity, guerrillas and social movements, especially in Central America and Latin America. Edith is the co-editor of the anthology *Feminisms in Movement: Theories and Practices from the Americas* (transcript 2023).

Ivo Zender is a PhD candidate in Linguistics and Literary Studies and Research Associate at the Interdisciplinary Center for Gender Research (IZG) at the University of Bielefeld. He holds an MA in European Literatures from the Humboldt-University of Berlin. His work is situated at the intersection of Queer/Trans and Literary Studies and he is writing his PhD dissertation on contemporary fictional trans literature.

Jannis Ruhnau is a PhD candidate in Sociology and Research Associate at the Interdisciplinary Center for Gender Research (IZG) at the University of Bielefeld. His research centres around Trans and Queer Studies, Feminist Studies, Affect Theory, Studies in Subjectivation, Queer Phenomenology and Discourse Analysis. His research interests include the lived and embodied experiences of trans and queer people as well as trans and queer cultures. His dissertation project focuses on the bodily becoming of trans and/or queer subjectivities in strength training. He is the author of the brochure *Teilhabe von trans* und nicht-binären Menschen am Sport* (Participation of trans* and non-binary people in sports) which was published in 2022 by Landeskoordination Netzwerk Geschlechtliche Vielfalt Trans* NRW.

Jules Joanne Gleeson is a queer historian and Londoner, based in Vienna. Her historical research has focused on pre-modern gender relations (especially Byzantine eunuchs), and the philosophy of revolutionary thought. She's written for publications including VICE, the Verso Books Blog, Pluto Press, Identities Journal, and Viewpoint Magazine, and performed internationally at a wide range of communist and queer cultural events. With Elle O'Rourke, Jules has edited the anthology *Transgender Marxism* (Pluto Press 2021), which is groundbreaking for a new trans* Marxist discussion. She is currently writing a new book titled *Hermaphrodite Logic: A History of Intersex Liberation*.

Lola Olufemi is a black feminist writer and Stuart Hall foundation researcher from London based in the Centre for Research and Education in Art and Media at the University of Westminster. Her work focuses on the uses of the feminist imagination and its relationship to cultural production, political demands and futurity. Her writing has been published by Afterall Journal, Architectural Review, Wasafiri Magazine, Stenberg Press, La Fabrique editions, Arcadia Missa, Lawrence and Wishart and others. She is author of *Feminism Interrupted: Disrupting Power* (Pluto Press 2020), *Experiments in Imagining Otherwise* (Hajar Press 2021) and a member of 'bare minimum', an interdisciplinary anti-work arts collective.

Sophie Lewis is a free-lance writer and independent scholar living in Philadelphia. Her first two books, both published by Verso, are *Full Surrogacy Now: Feminism Against Family* (2019) and *Abolish the Family: A Manifesto for Care and Liberation* (2022). Sophie's essays and articles appear in academic journals like Feminist Theory as well as magazines like the London Review of Books and newspapers like the New York Times. Sophie's PhD thesis, about gestational labor, is from Manchester University. Between 2007 and 2013, she studied English Literature (BA), then Environmental Theory (MSc), at Oxford University, followed by Politics (MA) at the New School for Social Research as a Fulbright Scholar. She now teaches short courses on critical theory, as a para-academic, at the Brooklyn Institute for Social Research. She also has an unpaid visiting affiliation with the Center for Research on Feminist, Queer and Transgender Studies at the University of Pennsylvania. You can find many of Sophie's lectures and writings at lasophielle.org, and become a subscriber at patreon.com/reproutopia. Her third book, *Enemy Feminisms*, is forthcoming at Haymarket in January 2025.

Vanessa Lara Ullrich is a PhD Candidate in Political Theory and the History of Ideas and Research Associate at the Interdisciplinary Center for Gender Research (IZG) at the University of Bielefeld. She studied Psychology and Politics at the Goethe-University of Frankfurt (B.Sc.) and the University of Oxford (M.Sc.). Her main research interests are critical theory and social philosophy. She also writes for newspaper outlets such as *Jacobin* or *Zeit Online*.

Verónica Gago is a professor for the Faculty of Social Sciences at Universidad de Buenos Aires and Universidad Nacional de San Martín, and she is a researcher at the National Scientific and Technical Research Council (CONICET). Her research focuses on international social movements, especially feminism and the critique of neoliberal reason. She is a prominent member of the feminist movement Ni una menos in Argentina. Some of her publications are: *Neoliberalism from Below: Popular Pragmatics and Baroque Economies* (Duke University Press 2017) *Feminist International: How to Change Everything* (Verso 2020). Together with Lucí Cavallero, she has published several texts on the topic of debt, among them: *A Feminist Reading of Debt* (Pluto Press 2021) and *The Home As Laboratory: Finance, Housing, and Feminist Struggle* (Common Notions 2024). Both of these books were translated by Liz Mason-Deese. Gago is also a member of the publishing house Tinta Limón Ediciones and writes regularly in various media outlets, especially in Latin America.

www.ingramcontent.com/pod-product-compliance
Lightning Source LLC
Jackson TN
JSHW051355060225
78516JS00003B/8